To those (that's YOU!) on the path to a purpose-filled life:
Your courage and wisdom inspires me every day.
Remember, the first step is to begin!

And, to Mick. Your love has touched me in ways I never knew
possible. Thank you for lighting my path this past year.

Succeed on Purpose
Everything Happens for a Reason

If you've ever wondered:

- If maybe you were on this Earth for a special reason, although you weren't sure what it was

- How to make the transition from doing what you know, to getting paid to do what you love

- How to use life's challenges to uncover your purpose

Then this book is for you.

Travel through the life of a young girl who always knew she had a purpose, although she didn't quite know what it was, much less how to get there.

You'll be inspired by her struggles and cheer her successes as teachers guide her through some of life's biggest obstacles. You'll celebrate her victories as she moves closer to her true purpose and destiny. Most importantly, through the powerful insights she experiences, you'll learn how to find your TRUE purpose and unleash the potential that's already within you.

Inspire on Purpose Books
909 Lake Carolyn Parkway
Suite 300
Irving Texas 75039

Visit our website at www.succeedonpurpose.com

ISBN: 978-0-9825622-9-1

First Printing: September 2010
10 9 8 7 6 5 4 3 2 1

SUCCEED ON PURPOSE
Everything Happens for a Reason

• • •

Terri Frey Maxwell

TABLE OF CONTENTS

Foreword – TRUTH: Everything Happens for a Reason

Chapter 1.   It Begins with Truth   9

Section 1 – ENDURANCE: A Child Learns to Survive

Chapter 2.   Purpose   17

Chapter 3.   God Will Show You the Way;
                You Have to Make the Way   23

Chapter 4.   Play to Win   29

Chapter 5.   Power in Restraint   37

Chapter 6   Don't Quit in the Middle of the Race   45

Chapter 7.   You Get What You Focus On   53

Section 2 – TRANSFORMATION: Survivor Into Thriver

Chapter 8.   Success is a Choice   65

Chapter 9.   You Get What You Give   71

Chapter 10.   Don't Try to Rule the World: Transform It   75

Chapter 11.   You Act Out What You Believe About Yourself   85

Chapter 12.   Succeed on Purpose   93

Chapter 13.   Forgiveness is a Blessing   99

Chapter 14.   Success is Not the Same as Purpose   109

Section 3 – PEACE: Build a Life on Purpose

Chapter 15.   Build a Life on Purpose   119

Chapter 16.   Find Your Purpose; Change Your Life   123

IT BEGINS WITH TRUTH

The Truth is...Everything
Happens for a Reason

My name is Terri Frey Maxwell and I was born to Laverne Stapleton and Dan Beeman, two teenagers who shared a weekend of passion in the summer of 1964. My father was in the Air Force and not interested in settling down when he received the call from my mother that she was pregnant with me. With nowhere to turn, my mother shared the news with her parents, who sent her in disgust to the Children's Home Society which had a program for girls "in this predicament."

The plan was simple. She would stay at the Home until she had given birth. Then the baby would be given up for adoption and a wonderful family would "raise it right." My mother wasn't given a choice in the matter. It was decided for her.

In a "closed" adoption, she would never get to meet her baby or the family who adopted it. Furthermore, she wasn't encouraged to bond with the baby because – as the nuns explained – it wasn't her child. It was God's child and would be given to a set of loving parents. They explained that she would not get to see, hold or nurse the baby. Upon birth, the nurses would be instructed to take the infant away and put the wheels in motion. Everything, including the adoption paperwork, would be handled ahead of time. After the birth, my mother would return to her life and try to forget that she had given away a child.

Although Laverne understood what she was being told to do, she still felt a connection to me, her unborn child. And against the advice of the nuns, she named me Danielle, after my father. Danielle. I love that name.

As my mother was being wheeled into the room where she would give me life, she reminded herself that this would be the birth of a child she would never hold. Her heart ached as she begged, "God, take care my baby. Please watch out for her because I can't."

At the conclusion of an agonizing birth, she thirsted for one thing: to hold her newborn child. As the physical pain subsided, it was quickly replaced by unbearable emotional pain as she felt her baby being taken away.

Panic set in. She screamed and pleaded to see me. The staff resisted, but the young girl who had always done exactly what she was told, briefly found a power inside her soul. Out of motherly instincts and sheer desperation, she sat up in her weakened state and demanded that they let her see me.

"Let me see her!" she said with a ferocity she'd never known. The nurses explained it was irreversible. The papers were signed. "I don't care. I want to see my child...RIGHT NOW!"

Against their better judgment, the nurses complied. From about three feet away, they held me up and then gently eased out the door.

My mother watched as I was taken away. A deafening silence fell over the room, only to be matched by an emptiness that filled Laverne's soul. She cried incessantly as the staff busied itself with cleanup duties, avoiding her pain.

Between sobs she said, "Danielle, you are special. God be with you."

Slowly the nurses rolled my tiny gurney down the hall with bright, translucent lights flipping by. As a newborn, I remember little except a vague notion that something felt like it had gone wrong and I wasn't where I was supposed to be.

That feeling hung over my life for decades. With newfound perspective, I imagine today that faintly in the distance, beyond the ability of the human eye to see, an angel appeared and escorted the nurses down the hall.

My life was about to take a course that no one could have predicted, but only God could have planned. Within moments of being born, when I should have been held safely in the arms of my birth mother, I would instead be whisked away by strangers. Rather than going home with the mother who gave me life, instead I would be taken to a children's home, randomly supervised while the match to my "new family" was made and legal proceedings completed.

I would soon be paired with a family that meant well, but was not equipped to support me. I would experience cruelty and anguish as I joined the millions of children who are victimized and learn to survive. Eventually, that survivor would learn to thrive and begin the process of fulfilling her purpose, just as God planned.

The story you're about to read is based on my life, although exactly what happened or when it happened isn't important. What really matters is what we do with what happens. Everything else is a perspective in time.

I was adopted from the Home by Darlene and Matthew Frey at about three months of age. The couple thought they couldn't have children, and had adopted a son two years before adopting me. They later had their own son, but that's a story for another time.

My adoptive parents had sincere intentions. Darlene really wanted children, almost as if she needed something to make her feel complete. The fact that she believed she was unable to have kids made the hole inside of her feel large.

Matthew was a fireman and Darlene was a stay-at-home mom. Everything seemed perfect for a while. They had the perfect little house, and now with two children, they had the perfect life. On the surface, that was true; underneath, not so much. A storm was brewing in our household. What started as young adults partying on the weekends quickly escalated into full-blown alcoholism which led to abuse: of themselves, each other and their children.

It is important to put the story in context. Although what happened after my adoption is not easy to absorb, know that I had angels, guides and everyday people who played an extraordinary role to lift and lead me to this place. Although some of what you will read in the early chapters is painful, the book isn't about pain. It's about hope. The story is meant to stimulate the hope that we all have deep inside of us, that everything that happens to us is truly part of a bigger plan. Everything that happens becomes what we make of it.

In the end, I hope to complete the circle of God's plan and live out that purpose in a powerful way. In spite of what happened, and in many ways because if it, I have a purpose and so do you. My purpose is to help you find yours.

As you read Danielle's story, it is the essence of her story that is important, and not the details. Understand that her lessons are absolutely true and that's what really matters. The lessons. What counts is not what happens to us, but what we do with what happens. Do we blame others for our misfortune, or do we turn that misfortune into a blessing? That's what the story is about: misfortune turned into a blessing and then into a purpose.

The best part about this story was the people who showed up, exactly when I needed them, with exactly the right words to comfort me and help me survive and eventually thrive. Their words and actions allowed me to fulfill my destiny.

Thank you, Gramps. You are my guardian angel even today. Thank you, Coach Dabney. I am alive today because of you. Thank you to my childhood neighbor, Pat Blessinger. Thank you to Uncle John, Aunt Carole and Uncle Rich. You believed in me when my own parents did not.

Thank you to my childhood friends and their families who nurtured me along the way: the Stinsons, the Stinnetts, the Walkers and the Cunninghams.

Thank you to my teachers: Ms. Frieda Gibson, Mrs. Patty Ballard, Mrs. Leslie Runnells, Mrs. Sally Smith, Dr. Karen Gray, Dr. Nancy Schreiber and Dr. Richard Miller.

Thank you to the mentors along the way: Burl Hogins, Alison Indrisano, Gregg McFarland, Sybil Williams, John Milton Fogg, Nido Qubein and Iyanla Vanzant. Thank you to the countless authors and coaches who have inspired me to become what I am destined to become.

And thank you to my parents: for Dan and Laverne who gave me life and the Freys who gave me roots. I will forever be grateful for your willingness to do the best you could. I promise to live up to my potential and to use my blessings to help others.

Everyone has a purpose. Everyone.

SECTION ONE

ENDURANCE: A Child Learns to Survive

CHAPTER

2

PURPOSE

Trust: Everyone Has
a Purpose

As the neon lights from the old city bar flickered against the windshield of her dad's beat-up van, Danielle looked out the window and wondered, "What am I doing here?" She found herself staring at the door intensely, willing it to open. She wanted nothing more than to see her father walk out of that bar so they could go home. "Why won't he come out?" The question filled her with despair.

She looked over at her older brother Jimmy, asleep on the van floor, and her younger brother, Mark. It was a school night and they were once again waiting for their father to leave the bar. It was almost ten o'clock and Danielle was tired. She didn't think this was what kids were supposed to be doing on a school night. Danielle really liked school and had grown dependent on the sense of routine it created in her otherwise chaotic world. Despite having a lot of friends, Danielle knew she was different. She didn't understand why, but she carried a heavy sense of responsibility. Sometimes it made her feel as if she didn't fit in with other kids, and quite often she felt alone.

Another hour ticked by without her father appearing. She fought back the urge to scream: "Daddy, where are you?!"

The blinking neon bar lights were hypnotic as they reflected in her wide eyes. She was tired, but fought sleep out of fear of what might happen if she did not stand watch over her brothers. Danielle knew she needed rest for school tomorrow, but there were too many questions swirling through her mind on this odd, starry night. Anguish washed over her as she replayed a life no child should ever have to experience.

"Why do my parents drink so much?" she questioned hopelessly. Her world was far from safe and she wondered why her parents didn't pay attention to their kids. It was as if she woke every morning abandoned. She lost track of how many nights she had fallen asleep hoping to awake in another place. How she longed to be with a family who really cared about her. "Who are these people? How could this have happened?"

Then came a question far too grave for a six-year old to ask: "How will we survive?" The children spent most of their evenings alone, figuring out how to prepare their own meals. When there was food in the house, it was a meager selection at best. Her father would come home with outdated, marked-down food from the discount grocery. She was too young to realize what this meant and often went to bed hungry.

Danielle glanced away from the lights and stared into the sky, hoping for relief from her frightening thoughts. She felt tired and sleepy. "Daddy, please..." she quietly begged.

As she gazed into the sky, she noticed a flash of light – almost like a UFO. She imagined Martians and space ships, even though she knew that the light was a shooting star. For some reason, the frightened little girl was more comfortable thinking about Martians than the inspiration of a star.

Danielle loved to think about other worlds, and found it calmed her down. She often daydreamed about visiting places she saw on TV, trying to escape the hopelessness of her young life. Tonight was no different. Slowly she faded off to sleep, with her head against the glass as the cool air swirled around the van windows. As she drifted off, Danielle made a wish upon that star. She sent a wish for God to bring her back to heaven where she belonged.

Suddenly, there was a bright glare, like a flashlight. The light was shining all around, but didn't appear to be pointed directly at her. She could see a glow from under her eyelids, yet it felt as if she was having a dream.

In her mind, she followed the light and the heat radiating from it. Danielle tried to open her eyes, but couldn't. She could feel someone watching her, although she couldn't seem to wake up. She wanted so badly to open her eyes to see what the light was.

Then she heard a voice call out to her, "Danielle, can you hear me?" It was a woman's voice. Her words were soothing. Danielle didn't recognize who it was, but instinctively knew it was coming from the light. "Yes," she said a bit afraid, "I can hear you."

"Danielle, I am your guardian angel," the voice said. "I am here to protect and guide you. You have been born for a very important reason."

Danielle began to experience a slight calmness, yet it was hard to keep from squirming. "Danielle, God specifically requested that I visit you this night in answer to the wish you sent earlier when you saw the star," the voice said.

Danielle couldn't believe it. "God heard me!" she said.

"Shhh," the angel said. "There is no need to wake. Just listen, child." The voice talked slowly and with purpose, which helped her pay attention. And in the voice was something foreign in her life so far -- the voice was filled with hope.

"Danielle, you were born to lead others, to inspire them, to show them the way, but your young life will be difficult. The challenges will prepare you to do something amazing. You will need to hold on to this hope." The voice was pleading with her. "You have to hold on to hope. Do you understand me, Danielle?"

Danielle nodded. Even at the age of six, she knew life was hard, yet she wanted to believe she was on Earth for something special. She wanted the hope the angel offered.

"Danielle, the years ahead will be very difficult," said the angel. "You have been placed with parents who are lost and will not be able to comfort you. Unfortunately, they are not equipped." The angel understood the doubt that lived inside the little girl, and chose words carefully to provide comfort. The words washed over Danielle...

...God would send people to help.

...She called them guides.

Danielle struggled to focus on the angel's request because she could see short clips of the challenges that lay ahead. The pictures were in fragments and not attached to the inevitable suffering to come, but Danielle could feel an immense burden. There was enough information in the angel's voice to tell her she had mountains to climb.

"Others will be sent to guide you, bringing insight and wisdom. Each lesson will be a gift to help fulfill your destiny. We need you to trust God. Can you do that, Danielle?"

Danielle's thoughts flashed to her "God tree" as she listened to the voice say, "God asks that you trust Him and pay close attention to the teachers he sends."

Danielle told the angel about her God tree – an old pine tree in the back yard – and how when she was confused or hurt, she climbed it and talked to God. She used the tree a lot, especially when her parents got angry. She would ask God to protect her.

"Good," said the angel. "Keep using the tree. Know that God is always there. When life is difficult, you can always go to Him. The teachers and guides will come in many different forms and will protect you and share wisdom. Do you understand me?"

Danielle thought she did. With her eyes still closed, she nodded and tried to smile.

"Danielle, know that you are loved, that you are important to God, and have been put here for a very important reason." Slowly, the light disappeared, as the angel's words trailed off. Gradually, Danielle opened her eyes. Then she looked around, somehow expecting a change in her surroundings – wishing she'd been taken to heaven. But she was still in the van and her brothers were still asleep. The neon light was blinking and her father remained in the bar. Nothing had changed for now, but there was a lingering sense of hope connected to the lone star that still twinkled brightly in the distance.

Now fully awake, Danielle wondered about what had happened. Was it a dream? What was she supposed to do? But at only six years old all she could feel was tired. Slowly, she drifted back to sleep, not knowing if the angel's visit was real or make-believe. Sometimes it was hard to tell.

The next thing she knew, the door to the bar flew open with a bang. Relief began to wash over her, "Finally!" She rubbed her eyes and sat up straight in the old seat of the van, expecting to see her dad stumble toward her. Disappointment grew tenfold when she realized it was another drunk and not her father. She sank back down and looked at the clock. It was after midnight. She was left with no choice but to take matters into her own hands.

Her mind flashed back to the angel, but she brushed the thought aside. All she could focus on was getting her family home.

Danielle climbed out of the van and walked through the lonely parking lot to the door of the old city bar. This would be the first of many times to come. She was still too tiny to negotiate the large door and found herself fighting back an overwhelming sense of despair as she tried to open it. This feeling was coupled with a huge sense of responsibility she could never escape, responsibility so strong it felt as if it would crush her under its weight.

Filled with resolve and drawing from something newly formed within her, she took a deep breath and gave a tug with everything she could muster. The door opened. It had begun.

CHAPTER

3

GOD WILL SHOW YOU THE WAY; YOU HAVE TO MAKE THE WAY

Surrender: Let go
and let God

Danielle found herself doodling in school. A phrase her grandpa had shared last weekend kept finding its way onto her paper: "God will show you the way; you have to make the way." She wondered if it must be an important idea.

The old man watched as his beautiful granddaughter played on the floor with her brother. He was certain the eight-year-old girl was special and was concerned that his very own son, Danielle's father, was a drunk. "How could my son treat his children like this?" he wondered. "I didn't raise him that way."

Something else was weighing on him. He had felt a "message" welling up in his heart every time Danielle was near. He didn't really understand what it meant and wasn't sure where the message came from, but felt he had to share it with her.

"Danielle, can you come here? Grandpa wants to tell you something." Without a word, the little girl bounded to his lap, placed her arms around his neck and snuggled next to

him. Danielle was fascinated with the way her grandpa spoke to her.

"Danielle, you know how I talk about God, and how if you trust Him he will take care of you? Well, there's more I want to tell you. God will always be there, he will always shine a light on the path, but you have to take it. You have to do the work. You have to respond to His light and take action. Does that make sense, sweetie?"

As Danielle was remembering this special time with her grandfather, her teacher asked the class to turn to a page in their spelling book. Danielle shut down her thoughts and threw herself at the assignment. Shortly thereafter, the bell rang and all the third-graders streamed out of the school, eagerly anticipating the weekend ahead.

Danielle's Saturdays were spent on household chores and babysitting her brothers. This weekend, however, wasn't turning out so well because her mom had been drinking and was angry that their father had stayed out all night. Around two in the afternoon, she loaded up the three kids in her car and said, "Come on, we're going down to the bar to find your dad."

Danielle hated these types of days, but was resigned to make the most of the situation. She told her brothers, "Hey, maybe we can play pinball," to make light of the impending doom they felt.

They could see their dad's van sitting near the door in its usual spot, as the car pulled into the parking lot of the bar. Once inside, the kids hurried off to play pinball and left their parents to squabble. The children got caught up in games and didn't pay attention to how drunk their parents had become.

It was dark outside when Danielle's father stormed out after an argument with her mom. An hour later, a cop came to the bar and informed them that their dad had gone to jail for driving while intoxicated. The cop instructed her mom to find another way home, because it was evident that she had been drinking also.

Danielle overheard the conversation as her mom argued with the policeman. She heard the cop say, "Ma'am, if you get in the car with those kids, you'll go to jail too and your kids will be sent to a foster home."

Danielle panicked. The thought of being taken away from her family was too much to bear. She knew they needed her desperately.

The officer made his way out of the bar and Danielle could hear her mom grumbling to her friends. As she knocked down another drink, she loudly protested, "That cop's not gonna tell me what to do." Danielle didn't understand what it all meant, but it couldn't be good.

About an hour later, the drunken woman hurried her kids through the dark parking lot and told them to get in the car. Danielle sensed danger. "Mom, don't. Can't we walk?" she pleaded, unaware they were miles away from home.

Her mom was belligerent. "Hell no! That damn cop ain't gonna tell me how to take care of my kids," she grumbled.

Danielle huddled in the back seat with her younger brother Mark as Jimmy took the front seat. The two older kids looked at each other with that all-knowing look of trepidation as they prepared themselves for what might come.

Soon the disaster unfolded. Her mom was unable to keep the car on the road and almost ran into a roadside barrier. The kids shrieked when it appeared they were going to crash. Jimmy and Danielle both pleaded, "Mom, pull over, OK?"

The car plunged toward the shoulder and finally came to rest at the edge of a steep trench. Her mom got out of the car and started hollering about the "damn car that ran me off the road." Then she passed out at the rear of the vehicle, near the back tire. The two older children jumped out of the car when her body hit the ground. They stared in disbelief at the sight of their mother lying against the car. The words of the police officer rang in Danielle's ears: "foster home."

Jimmy gasped, "Danielle, what are we going to do?" Although he was two years older, Jimmy always turned to Danielle in times of trouble. The words came out of her mouth in a quiver, "I don't... know...Jimmy."

Danielle felt her desperation escalate. Her biggest concern was that the cops would take them away. She could not let that happen. She believed that it was her job to keep the family together and worked constantly to take care of everyone. Danielle secretly feared that someday the family would fall apart and she would be helpless to do anything about it. Now it seemed that moment was near.

She knew they had to find a way home before the police officer found them. With her resolve fortified, the young girl began to focus on the problem.

They were not far from home now. She tried to wake her mom, thinking they could leave the car and walk. After several attempts, it became clear that her mom wasn't waking up anytime soon. Danielle wanted to throw a complete and utter fit right there on the side of the road. She did not want this responsibility! It was not fair! She was tired of her parents' behavior!

In spite of her anger, her sense of responsibility compelled her to assume the role of guardian once again.

"Jimmy, we have to get her inside the car before the cops find us."

They had carried their parents inside the house before, so they immediately jumped into the routine. Jimmy came around and the two youngsters tugged and pulled. It took every effort the children had to move their mother from the ground to the car. Every minute that passed was like a lifetime of worry all bottled up in one big dreadful package. They could now add this to the many moments in which they were required to manage a situation beyond their years.

With her mom in the back seat and the car door shut, Danielle wiped the sweat from her eyes and hurried her brothers into the front seat in hopes they would not be seen by the traffic that zoomed by. She was tired and overwhelmed. Danielle knew she had to figure out how to get home as she stared out the windshield hopelessly, not knowing what to do. She bowed her head and prayed, "God...help me."

Suddenly, Grandpa's words came back to her. "God will show you the way; you have to make the way." She gently closed her eyes and prayed for God to show her what to do.

With her eyes closed, she could see a light and with it came a powerful feeling. It was a feeling she had never experienced. God asked her to surrender and trust. Danielle struggled with this for a second, until she heard the phrase again, "God will show you the way; you have to make the way."

So, she let go and trusted. With child-like faith, she gave control to God and asked him to show her what to do. Within seconds a scene played out in her head, like a movie. Instantly, she knew what she had to do. It was a gift that filled her with hope. She found herself feeling thankful for the first time all evening. They might actually have a chance!

"Jimmy, here's the deal. We have to get Mom home, and the only way we can do that is to drive this car. Let's put Mark on the floor so he can press the gas pedal, and I want you to get up on your knees and steer. I will sit here and watch for traffic and make sure we're going the right way."

Jimmy thought the concept sounded ridiculous, but didn't have any other ideas. He could sense by his sister's voice that getting home was important. He loved the thought of driving anyway, and had always wanted to sit on Dad's lap and steer the van.

While Jimmy was thinking through the plan, Danielle showed Mark how to work the gas pedal. She was on the floor with him, demonstrating how to press the pedal lightly and to let off when she told him.

Softly, Danielle kept whispering the phrase, "God will show you the way; you have to make the way." The words comforted Jimmy as he watched his younger brother get into position on the floor below him.

With an uncanny steadiness, the kids slowly moved the car off the side of the road. Fortunately, traffic had thinned out. Moving at about 10 miles an hour, they eased the car toward home. Danielle directed and encouraged her brothers. When they started going too fast, she told Mark to "ease off the gas, Mark," until they coasted back to 10-15 miles an hour.

Jimmy was amazed as they neared their street. He was proud of himself, and couldn't wait to tell his friends. He was proud of Danielle too, and loved that she kept repeating, "God will show you the way, you have to make the way," as they eased the car down their street.

Once into the driveway, Danielle rushed her brothers into the house and took a blanket out to her mom, leaving her there until she woke – whenever that would be.

Although she was proud of how well they had worked together, there was a growing seed of anger that was flourishing deep within her. She brushed it aside and made sure her brothers were safely in their beds.

Drifting off to sleep, she smiled at the thought of sitting on her grandfather's lap and hearing the words that she had used tonight. For a few seconds, right before her eyes closed, she could feel hope wash over her again. "God will show you the way: you have to make the way," she whispered. Maybe God would watch out for her after all.

CHAPTER

4

PLAY TO WIN

Awareness: We Become
What We Fight

Danielle loved softball. It meant being outside and playing with friends. She loved everything about it – the physical activity, the team spirit, the thrill of winning. Softball was one of the few ways she could escape and enjoy life.

It was the playoffs. She'd pestered her parents for more than a week to come to the game and watch her play. They rarely watched her games, but she thought the playoffs would be different. Her team was really good, and Danielle was one of the best players in the league.

Deep down, Danielle didn't expect her parents to come, but she fantasized about hitting a home run and having them cheer her around the bases. She continued to remind them of the game, but they were disinterested in anything that did not revolve around their own personal needs.

As she rode her bike to the field, she wondered if they would show up. Her imagination was in full force as she glided up the sidewalk and stopped to lean her bike against the fence. The gate to the field was open and once she passed through the entrance, she spotted her friends. Lisa saw Danielle and lofted the ball high into the air in her direction. Danielle took off after it and imagined running for a fly ball and a game-winning catch. As she continued to warm up with her teammates, she kept thinking "I hope they come!"

With the game about to begin, her parents were nowhere in sight. Danielle trotted out to third base, trying to lift her spirits, smiling and joking with her friends as she continued to scan the bleachers. Then a surprise... before the first pitch, Danielle saw her dad's truck pull into the parking lot.

"Oh my God, Dad's here!" She could hardly contain her excitement. She turned away from him toward the outfield and gathered up her emotions as she put on her game face for the big day ahead. Then she posed in her very best third-base stance so he could see it. She smiled and waited.

Danielle quickly realized something was very wrong. As she watched her dad stumble out of the truck, she shrank inwardly, knowing this day would play out much differently than she had imagined. He was drunk again. Within seconds of that realization, she remembered where they were.

"Oh no!" she said out loud to herself. "Not here. Not in front of my friends!"

She was crushed. Danielle put her ball glove up against her face and felt the heat from her entire body rush up into her cheeks and start to burn. She kept thinking, "I can't believe this, I can't believe this is happening!"

It was well into the first inning before Danielle was able to pull herself out of the nightmare unfolding in her mind to realize that she was still standing on the field. Fortunately, no one hit the ball in her direction. She was lost in an array of dreadful thoughts. She wanted to race from the field in utter dismay. She stood there helplessly and tried not to choke on the fear of what was to come.

The first inning ended. Danielle's team was up to bat.

Danielle was third in the batting lineup. As she neared the plate, her dad started screaming wildly, "You better get a hit, Danielle! You better get a hit! I'm gonna kill you if you don't get a hit!" The parents around him suddenly got quiet. A lot of fathers got excited and yelled at their kids, but this was different: he sounded mean. The other parents were shocked at his cruelty. Danielle felt a deep humiliation. She wanted to melt, or dig a hole under home plate and crawl in it until the game was over. She stood at home plate, shaking. Three strikes later, it was over. She had struck out.

Immediately her dad said, "You're stupid, you're terrible. I can't believe they don't put you on the bench!" The other parents were appalled at what they heard. It was clear by the look on their faces that his behavior disturbed them. Danielle walked away with her head down, ashamed.

Coach Stinnett walked up to Danielle and took her aside. He put his arm around her consolingly. "You OK?" he asked.

Danielle shrugged him off, acting tough. "Leave me alone and let me play the game," she thought to herself. As her teammates focused on the player up to bat next, Danielle could only replay her terrible performance. How could she strike out? Her embarrassment grew.

As her resentment took shape, she thought, "I'm gonna show him. I'm gonna beat him. I'm gonna show him that I am better than he is!" She was spoiling for a fight now, as something razor-sharp ran through her veins.

Her team quickly secured three outs against its opponent, but Danielle did not have a chance at bat for a few more innings. It was as though time had slowed to a painful pace, which made Danielle even angrier. When she finally did get her chance at bat, her rage had intensified. She was determined to beat her father like there was no tomorrow and make him look like a fool.

She stood at the plate waiting for the pitcher to throw, and imagined ripping the cover off the ball. The pitch was right across the plate and a little low, and Danielle swung so hard that she fell to her knees. Her dad started howling. "Oh, you can't hit anything!" he mocked. "I don't know why they don't put you on the bench, you couldn't hit a thing!" The crowd grew silent again as they watched shame wash over the young girl's face.

Danielle grimaced, her face growing hotter. Knowing she had to prove him wrong, she stepped up to the plate slowly, took a breath and focused. She was simply going to knock the ball into outer space and shut his mouth with one giant swing.

Two strikes later, disabled by her fury, she had struck out again. It was the first time in years that Danielle had struck out two times in a row. She threw down her helmet and her bat. Danielle had a quick temper, but now she was totally out of control.

Coach Stinnett grabbed her by her shirt and jerked her behind the dugout. "What are you doing?" he said. "You're not playing to win, you're playing to fight!"

She was visibly shaking, as she stared down her coach with teeth and fists clenched.

"You're not thinking about the game, and you're not thinking about the team. All you're thinking about is getting even with your dad. You are not playing to win. If you want to be a champion, you have to play to win!"

His words echoed in her head, and Danielle knew this was an important moment. She continued to wrestle with his words against the backdrop of her own anger. Her coach calmed down and put both hands on her shoulders.

He looked her in the eye and said, "You can't control your dad any more than you can control the weather." With an incredible amount of love and compassion, he added, "Or the hand that life has dealt you."

He hugged her and held her close for a second as she squirmed. Then, sensing what she needed, he told her how important she was to him and to the team. He waited until she stopped fighting her internal battle before pushing her out on the field with a gentle slap on the back. His words rang in her mind. He was right.

She didn't know how to turn off the rage that enveloped her entire body, so she did the only thing she knew how to do: she opened her heart in prayer.

Standing right there on third base, Danielle prayed, "God, release me from this anger, please cleanse it from me. Let it flow out of me and replace it with your love and the desire to win instead of fight."

The crack of a bat drew Danielle's attention away from her prayers. A fly ball was sailing high into the air in her direction. If she could catch this ball, it would be a step toward redeeming herself. Right before the ball landed in her glove, she remembered picturing the game-winning catch during warm-up. Smack. The ball landed in her glove and she instantly felt relief as her teammates congratulated her.

Soon it was the last inning and her team had its final chance to string together enough hits. The game was close, with Danielle's team one run behind and at bat. There was a runner on first, a runner on second and two outs.

Danielle would have one more chance.

With a decent hit, she could drive in two runs and win the game. She blocked out the sounds of her father ranting in the background. The rest of the crowd was silent. It was a crucial moment. Their hearts ached for the girl and many onlookers prayed for her to overcome the challenge placed before her.

Danielle stood at home plate and glanced over at her team and coach. She knew they believed in her. She told herself it did not matter what her dad said because each and every one of her teammates needed her to be a champion at that moment. They needed her to play to win.

Danielle stepped up to the plate and the first pitch came in solidly. She whacked it over the pitcher's head, over the center fielder's head, and took off for first base. The first runner came in, and then the second. She was elated as she ran the bases, watching her teammates score ahead of her.

The outfielders were trying to recover the ball, and at every failed attempt she grew stronger and more certain of herself. As she turned toward third base, Coach Stinnett was jumping up and down: "You did it!"

When she finally placed her foot on third base, the game now won, tremendous joy and a deep appreciation replaced the burden she had been carrying. She had done it! She had led her team to victory. Danielle looked over at her father. The crowd was cheering wildly, except for him. Danielle looked up to the sky and said, "Thank you, God." Then she turned to her coach and said defiantly, "I play to win!"

After the game, Coach Stinnett pulled her aside. He knew the excitement would wear off and Danielle would once again feel the pain and embarrassment of her father's actions. He felt compelled to help her understand the importance of the lesson shared. His words now seemed to brim with hope.

Coach Stinnett said, "Danielle, my whole life, all I knew was how to fight. I like to win, but I learned the hard way that if I'm not careful, I become what I fight. When I saw you strike out the second time, I saw a champion become the rage she fought against. I knew you were better than that. When you focused on winning, and not beating your father, you lifted up yourself and your team. It's a wonderful lesson that I hope you don't forget."

Danielle smiled and promised she would not forget. Then she raced over, jumped on her bike, and pedaled in the direction of home. As she flew down the street, she replayed the events of the day and remembered how she overcame disappointment and failure.

Danielle could still feel the rage burning inside, so she tucked her coach's words in her heart and smiled. "I play to win." For a brief minute, hope returned.

CHAPTER 5

POWER IN RESTRAINT

Power: He Who Controls
Others May Be Powerful,
But He Who Has
Mastered Himself Is
Mightier Still (Lao Tzu)

Over the next few years, everything went progressively downhill; spiraling out of control. While most kids were enjoying their teenage independence, Danielle was busy holding the pieces of her fractured family together. At 13, she was a wreck.

Her father lost his job, and a life that was already difficult now became dreadful. He picked up some occasional construction work, but without a strict work routine he had even more time to drink. One thing was for sure: alcohol had a spell on their family. Things were falling apart and Danielle could do nothing to stop it.

Her mom cleaned houses to earn extra money, but this contribution wasn't enough. Danielle mowed lawns, baby-sat and did odds and ends for the neighbors to earn lunch and spending money. She could tell her family's financial situation was precarious, although she didn't imagine how much worse it was about to get.

At the end of her eighth-grade year, her father sold their house and moved the family to a dilapidated trailer in a little fishing community 30 minutes north of where she had grown up. The trailer was less than 600 square feet, with five people living there. Her older brother, Jimmy, frequently disappeared for days on end, and when he was home, he slept on the floor.

The trailer had two small bedrooms, each with barely enough room for a bed and a closet. The bedrooms were connected by a hallway and tiny bathroom, and the rest of the space held the kitchen and living room. There was talk of purchasing a second trailer and connecting it so the family would have more room, but Danielle couldn't envision how that would help, because the problem seemed to be more than physical space.

The trailer was old and falling apart like her life. Worse, it was infested with cockroaches and occasionally a rat would make itself known. It felt like a bad dream.

"How could this be happening?" Danielle wondered. "And why am I the only person who thinks there is something wrong with how we are living? Doesn't anyone notice the roaches and the rats?" Her younger brother made a game out of swatting the bugs, somehow thinking it was funny. The roach infestation was so bad that at night Danielle could hear the dirty bugs running across her wall posters. She would tuck her covers tightly around her body and pull them over her head so she could sleep protected.

Danielle's family accepted its living conditions almost as easily as a change in the weather. It didn't make sense to the teenager, who now felt more unsafe than at any point in her life. She was frequently shocked to find dishes in the sink with bugs crawling all over them.

The pain of the physical relocation was compounded by the fact that Danielle had to leave her friends, her beloved softball team and her God tree. She would soon be in a new high school away from everything familiar. She had never felt this alone, ever. Many nights she would lie in her tiny bed and cry herself to sleep.

One summer night, a few hours after Danielle had gone to

bed, she heard her father's van drive up. She could tell he'd had too much to drink before he even made it through the front door. She lay perfectly still.

As he stumbled through the kitchen and into the hallway, she heard him unbuckle his belt. He was mumbling incoherently. Before she knew it, she felt the full weight of her father on top of her, with his pants down around his knees. She could feel his unshaven face brushing against hers, and smell the stench of whisky on his breath. She wanted to vomit.

Her father had touched her when he was drunk before and sometimes he used to come into the bathroom when she was in the shower and look at her, making comments about her body. Sometimes he showed her pictures of naked women, telling her that she would grow up to "look like this." He had exposed himself and had touched her in ways that were wrong. It felt gross, and all she could do was wait for him to stop.

But there was something different about what he was doing now. It was more than touching. She could feel the fright build in her chest as her father wiggled his semi-naked body on top of her.

Danielle didn't know what was happening, but she knew it was worse than what had come before. With all of her might, and a power she had never known, she pulled up her knees and lifted him enough so that she could put her hands on his chest. And then, with one swift motion, she pushed her hands and lifted her legs like a catapult machine. Her father flew off her and crashed into the closet door before sliding onto the floor, his pants still around his knees. Her mom heard the commotion from her bed a few feet away, and came into the hallway. She said, "What the hell?" as she saw him slumped on the floor with his pants down, and in the backdrop of the moonlight shining through a window, saw her teenage daughter huddled against the wall in terror.

Without uttering another word, her mother picked him off of

the floor and carried him to their bedroom, tossing his body onto the bed in utter disgust.

Danielle could still smell the liquor hanging over the room. She touched her cheek which burned from where his unshaven face had rubbed against hers. In spite of the pain, she wrapped herself in the newfound idea that she could take care of herself. After a few hours, she drifted off to sleep.

The next morning she woke to someone making French toast and bacon for breakfast. The smell of the food brought back good memories of a long time ago. Danielle bounded out of bed to rush into the kitchen. Before she reached her bedroom door, she remembered the night before and stopped dead in her tracks. "Was it a dream?" she wondered. "Did that really happen?" She looked around the room for evidence, but could find none.

After a few moments, she decided that it didn't matter, and rested on the notion that she would never again let him touch her, look at her or make obscene comments to her. "Never again," she declared.

Slowly, she headed down the small hall into the kitchen. Her mom greeted her with a smile and said, "Hi, honey. I made you breakfast." Danielle was dumbfounded. "Wow, uh..." and let her words drift off as she sat at the small table in the kitchen.

As her mom served her breakfast, Danielle really started to worry. "What the hell?!" she wondered. No one had served her breakfast for as long as she could remember.

As Danielle ate, her mom opened the conversation. "Honey, your dad is still asleep. He came home drunk again last night. I guess he must have mistaken your room for the bathroom because he pulled down his pants to pee, but he was in your room and not the bathroom." And then she gave off this little chuckle like it was funny.

Danielle sat perfectly motionless, now fully immersed in the realization that what happened last night, did indeed happen. Her mom continued, "Yeah, he's done that before. Pulled down his pants and mistaken the bed for the toilet. That's what he gets for drinking so much."

And with that, Danielle's mom dismissed the event and changed the subject entirely, asking questions about Danielle's new school, as if nothing had happened.

Danielle slowly got up, put her plate in the sink, changed her clothes, and headed out the door to her neighbor's house. There was fire in her belly as her brain fumbled with the notion that her mother had simply and irrevocably justified her father's abusiveness and dismissed it so casually.

She was conflicted by the realization that she was totally alone, yet empowered by the awareness that she could protect herself. She decided to focus on that power and let it pour over her. She imagined herself like the Incredible Hulk, growing huge muscles and tearing down everything in sight.

About that time, she saw her next-door neighbor's cat coming toward her. The rage seethed in her, burning in the pit of her stomach. She looked at the cat, and then kicked it yowling across the driveway of her neighbor's house.

"Danielle! What are you doing?!" her neighbor yelled, bursting out of her door and comforting the cat. "You should be ashamed!"

Michelle and Bill Cooper had taken a liking to Danielle. Michelle would make cookies and give her soda in the afternoon. Her own daughter had left for college a year earlier and she liked having Danielle around. Even with her fondness for the teen, this behavior was unacceptable.

Danielle fumed as Michelle stared at her. She wanted to hit something. She saw a plant in a ceramic pot, swung it up above her head and smashed it on the floor. Her eyes were filled with rage as she waited to see what Michelle would do.

Michelle slowed her speech to a soft tone, hoping not to further ignite the firestorm brewing in the troubled teen. "Danielle, what's wrong?" she pleaded softly.

Danielle turned around looking for the next thing she could throw. Michelle was concerned the situation would escalate out of control. A phrase flashed into her mind and came out of her mouth unexpectedly.

"There is power in restraint." After hesitating a second, she added, "True power is the power to control oneself, Danielle." She waited and then added more forcefully, "Stop what you are doing, right now!"

Danielle stopped. Rage emptied from her body and was quickly replaced by tears. Years of abuse and anger came pouring out and the tears soon became a flood. She wept in convulsive waves in the older woman's arms, who in turn gently rocked her back and forth.

Finally Danielle said, "Michelle, I am so sorry. I am tired of living, and so tired of trying to make everything OK. I guess I feel like if I don't start fighting, I'll die. That if I am not strong, I will be a helpless victim forever."

Although Michelle had no idea what had caused the outburst, she wanted desperately to ease the girl's pain. She held Danielle and stroked her head gently until she could feel the tension leave the teen's body.

"Danielle, Lao Tzu said, 'There is nothing stronger than gentleness.' He was a Chinese philosopher who thought that it was only through self-restraint that we learn how to use power for good. He taught that true power is like water. There is nothing more submissive or moldable than water, yet attacking water is futile because it is completely elusive. To find your power, you must be like water. For as Lao Tzu said, 'He who controls others may be powerful, but he who has mastered himself is mightier still.'"

Danielle didn't quite understand what she was saying, but could sense the peace in Michelle's words.

Michelle said, "Picture your favorite body of water, Danielle. What is it?"

Danielle thought for a second, and a picture-perfect image flashed into her mind. It was a beach on the Florida Gulf that she had visited with one of her friends, Sheila, when she was in elementary school. "Siesta Key Beach," she said. "That's my favorite place in the world."

The older woman said, "Picture that beach. Do you see how powerful the waves are, yet how peaceful they are at the same time? That's true power, Danielle. Peaceful strength – like the waves of the ocean. Rather than fighting what's around them, they flow with it effortlessly. But, never, ever, do the waves lose their power. Be like those waves, Danielle."

And with that, she helped Danielle up and eased her into the house. She gave her cookies and soda, and gently wiped away her dirt-stained tears with a cold washcloth. She let the love she felt for the girl spill out of her with every stroke of the soft washcloth.

After a while, Danielle got up to go, thanked Michelle and again apologized, assuring her it would never happen again.

"There is power in restraint," Danielle repeated to herself as she walked home. She wasn't sure how that would help her survive, but the love she felt from Michelle, in stark contrast to her own anger, was cemented in her mind, along with the vision of the ocean and its powerfully peaceful waves – – waves that reminded her of the power inside, a power so strong it could crumble rocks and yet so peaceful it could bring a soul to rest on its shores.

CHAPTER
6

DON'T QUIT IN THE MIDDLE OF THE RACE

Perspective: Failure is a
Perspective That Changes
With Time

The phone rang as Danielle was beginning her homework. Jimmy got up and answered it. There was a look of panic on his face as he hung up.

"Come on, we have to go get Dad," he said.

Danielle was pissed. "Not again," she fumed.

Jimmy said, "It's bad. He passed out behind a dumpster. Billy Raskin found him.

"Oh, no..." Danielle shrieked. Billy Raskin was on the boy's basketball team.

The two teenagers worked out the plan. Danielle would talk to Billy and get the story, and Jimmy would assess the damage. Then they'd load their dad into the truck and Jimmy would drive him home, leaving Danielle to drive the van.

As soon as the kids pulled into the Winn Dixie grocery parking lot, they knew where to go. Their dad frequently would grab old food from the dumpsters that had been thrown away by the store and bring it home for the family to eat.

As they quickly worked their way to the back of the grocery store, they saw their dad's van with the headlights pointing toward the dumpster. Although it was dusk, they could see him, asleep, passed out right there next to the dumpster with stale bread in his hand.

Fifteen-year-old Danielle went over to Billy and asked what had happened, trying to pretend that this wasn't a regular occurrence.

"I don't know what happened, man. I came out and found him here. I thought you should know." It was all he would offer. Billy helped them lift the drunken old man and put him in the truck. He added, "Hey guys, I am sorry. Let me know if there's anything you need."

Danielle was relieved that he hadn't made a bigger deal out of it. Everything else went as planned, and soon the kids had their dad home in bed and Danielle returned to her homework.

The next day, Danielle bounded toward her first-period classroom, naively ignorant of the firestorm brewing. She walked in as the last bell rang and took her seat, oblivious to the smirks of the girls who sat near her.

Within minutes, Danielle noticed that three girls were passing around a piece of paper and laughing. She glanced over at Amy Raskin, her basketball teammate and friend. Amy had an odd look on her face. She held on to a piece of paper in one hand and tapped the shoulder of the girl in front of her. Danielle was confused. It slowly dawned on her that Billy Raskin, the boy who had found their father the night before, was Amy's brother. A familiar sense of doom quickly surrounded her, almost choking off her breath.

As her fate became clear, Danielle saw the paper the girls were passing around. It was a hand-made sign with the words

"Danielle, what's for dinner?" scribbled on it in magic marker.

"Oh my God," Danielle thought. They all knew. They all knew. How would she ever live this down? She agonized in disbelief and prayed this was part of a bad dream from which she desperately wanted to wake up.

The day went downhill from there. It didn't take long before her teammates and many other kids had heard about her father's latest stunt. Although the shame of her father's actions was a part of life she tried not to think about, the betrayal of her friends was like a double-edged sword. She literally felt sliced open and vulnerable.

Danielle sought out her brother Jimmy at lunch. "Hey man, we're screwed," Danielle sighed as she plopped down next to her brother. It was clear from his face that Jimmy knew what she was talking about. For some reason the older boy wasn't concerned. He said "Look, they'll forget about it by tomorrow. Don't let it bother you."

Danielle wished she could be so carefree. All day the taunts continued. Everywhere she went, someone had something to say. The shame and hurt manifested into rage; it burned inside her, and filled her with an anger she could no longer stand.

With every remark, it felt like another cut into her heart, reminding her of all of the pain she had endured. It wasn't long before she was lost in a constant stream of hurtful memories replaying in her mind. Overwhelmed by a tumultuous life viciously replayed this morning, Danielle started to picture the most horrifying ways to prevent herself from seeing another day.

By fifth period, she was trying desperately to focus on inspirational words others had shared to help overcome the strife, but with every cruel comment, those lessons fell flat and evaporated into nothingness.

It was too much. So... she decided. She would end it all that very night. It had been this way for so long and the teenager simply could not picture any other way to escape. Even if God Himself gave her a guarantee that things would get better, she would not believe it. There appeared to be no end to the suffering and she was completely without hope.

Being repeatedly humiliated by her classmates was bad, but by her basketball teammates was the worst. By the time practice rolled around, Danielle had cemented the dreaded decision to take her life that night, and had crafted a detailed plan. She would miss Gramps terribly, but even his love could not repair the brokenness she felt. She was certain nothing could. She couldn't handle the pressure, the embarrassment or the nagging responsibility. She wanted out, and wanted out now. Out of this life for good. Feeling more and more insignificant as the day dragged on, she was convinced no one would miss her.

Walking into the gym for practice, she grabbed a ball and went to the side court to shoot free throws, as far away from her teammates as she could get. She wanted nothing to do with them, and only wanted to escape the hell that surrounded her.

Danielle slammed the ball into the ground, transferring her anger onto the ball. Immersed in her misery, she didn't hear her guidance counselor, Coach Dabney, come up behind her.

"Hey Danielle, how's it going?" he asked.

"Fine," she lied, focused only on getting through the next few hours so she could go home and end it all.

"Danielle, we need to talk. I heard about what happened and I know you must be at the end of your rope," he said. Danielle was shocked. "How did he know?" she wondered. "Did he really understand how far down the rope she was?"

"Look at those girls over there," Coach Dabney said. Danielle refused to acknowledge the so-called teammates who had played out her personal hell for the whole school to see. Instead, she pulled away and slammed the ball against the wall.

"Danielle, listen to me. Of the 10 players on this team, only six will graduate from this school. Of those six who graduate, three will go to college and only one of those will graduate with a degree. Those are the hard facts. One in 10 of our students graduates from college. You are smart enough to be the one who makes it, Danielle. You have what it takes. You're smart, driven and wise. But if you end it now, you'll never win the race."

"Huh?" Danielle said, now starting to pay attention. "What race, coach?"

"Well, if you think of life like a race, you're not even to the middle of the race. If you quit now, you'll never know where you could have finished." He let the words hang in the air for effect and added, "Think about it this way. Take a look at the scoreboard over there. Would you stop playing the game at halftime?"

"No, I guess not, coach, but I thought they were my friends."

"Danielle, people can be mean. But look at those girls over there. Take a good hard look. None are as smart as you. None have the potential you have. The reason those girls were so quick to kick you when you were down is because they know they don't have what you have."

He continued, "Success and failure are perspectives we possess during a snapshot in time. The question is whether you quit right now or finish the race to someday gain the perspective of how this adversity will help you realize your potential."

Danielle was shocked. She'd never thought about it like that. She never thought of herself as being smarter than other kids. She constantly felt like a failure because of how desolate her life was.

"Danielle, you can't quit in the middle of the race, or you'll never know what you're made of. We only fail when we refuse to try. Stay in the race, Danielle. I'll bet in 20 years you will accomplish more than all of those girls who are making fun of you today put together. But, if you quit on life..." He left the words in the air for her to grasp.

She thanked him as he slapped her on the shoulders and told her to get back to practice, then nodded to her basketball coach, who was watching from a distance.

As Danielle ran next to her teammates, she thought about the message Coach Dabney had spoken. She was thankful he had taken time to comfort her and was amazed at how instinctively he knew the thoughts that filled her mind. Growing weary of the life that surrounded her, she had considered taking her life many times the last few years. This time was different. As a sophomore in high school, she felt like there was no other way to escape. And she wanted to escape.

Danielle considered his words again as she ran sprints: "Don't quit in the middle of the race..." "Success and failure are perspectives..."

She didn't know if Coach Dabney really understood her despair, but his kindness gave her enough courage to get through practice and the night ahead. Although she couldn't embrace the sense of hope that had comforted her as a child, by the time she jumped off the bus the next morning and headed for class, she felt a little stronger. She wondered if maybe she had something to offer. If Coach Dabney thought she was smart, maybe she was. She kept thinking about his metaphor of the race. She pictured hurdles she had already jumped, and hurdles that remained ahead. She pictured herself in charge of her own race, that somehow she could determine the victory.

She wanted the nagging doubt to be converted to confidence as she replayed the words, "Don't quit in the middle of the race, Danielle.

Success and failure are only perspectives taken at a point in time."

She had an idea. As she walked into class, she grabbed the dictionary off the shelf and looked up the word "failure." Webster's stated that failure was "failing to perform a duty or expected action."

"Wait a minute," she thought. "I've never failed. I've always done what I was supposed to do, even though the outcome wasn't always what I wanted." About that time, Coach Dabney stuck his head into the room and nodded to her teacher, Mrs. Ballard, that he wanted to speak to Danielle.

"Danielle, how are you doing? I came to check on you."

"I'm better coach, but I have a question. What is failure? I feel that all of my challenges in life, these things that are out of my control, mean that I am worthless, that I can never win."

"Danielle, failure isn't about winning or losing. We only fail when we don't try. Our society confuses losing with failure. When we give something everything we can, and it doesn't work out the way we wanted, it doesn't mean we failed. It means that God has a different plan, and we have to trust Him. You can only control your actions. The outcome is up to God."

"But coach, how can I succeed when I keep getting pulled back down?" Danielle asked with defeat in her voice.

Coach Dabney carefully chose each word, knowing how important it was to help her tap into the belief in herself that he held each time he watched her persevere.

"Everything that happens leads to a perspective, and you get to choose which perspective you take each moment. You can choose to believe you are a victim of what happens, or you can choose to believe that you will survive what happens and are being prepared for something better. You can choose right now whether or not you will overcome the hand you've been dealt this week, or you can choose to quit. Choose the perspective you want to take, for it is nothing more than that – a perspective." With a smile, he turned and walked away.

Right then, something shifted in Danielle. The anger was still inside, but a seed of confidence had been planted. As she returned to her seat, she thought, "Maybe I am somebody. Somebody who was meant to do something."

For the time being, she put away her doubt and focused on her chosen perspective. "I choose to believe I am being prepared for something better." She liked how it sounded and how it felt.

For a fleeting moment, a bright light appeared in her mind, reminding her of a vision long time ago. Reminding her of a dream and a promise. Reminding her that she was indeed here for a reason. It was an angel's light.

CHAPTER

7

YOU GET WHAT YOU FOCUS ON

Focus: Energy Flows
Where Attention Goes

Danielle strutted into the gym. It was an important playoff game and at 17, she loved being the starting point guard. During the first half, Danielle played her best game all year. Her team was much faster in the open court and ran up the score using a fast break that allowed Danielle's speed, athleticism and ball-handling abilities to shine.

She delighted in the cheers from the crowd and the praise from teammates each time she led a play that resulted in a score. By halftime, the 11th grader was on top of the world. "Game on!" she said as she waltzed onto the court for the second half, cocky and ill-prepared for what was about to happen.

The other team had made a major adjustment at halftime, having paid close attention to how Danielle's team moved the ball down the court.

At the start of the second half, Danielle grabbed the ball and drove down the court. Two opposing players waited as she crossed half court on the right side and quickly moved into a formation called a "trap." Danielle lost the ball to the defenders, who in turn quickly scored.

She was furious! Danielle took the ball and this time ran straight toward the defenders, convinced that if she was a little faster she could get past the defenders who were again poised to set a trap. This time, instead of driving toward them, Danielle made the mistake of stepping backward after they had formed the trap. The referee blew the whistle. She knew better than to step backward across the court because it was an illegal move, resulting in the ball being turned over to the opposing team, which then scored.

Danielle fumed. "I'll try harder this time, I'll show them, I'll get by them," she thought. This time she ran even faster down the court, and as soon as the defenders stepped up into the trap, she ran straight at them, but failed to squeeze between them before it was fully set.

The referee blew his whistle, charging Danielle with an offensive foul, which again put the ball into the opposing team's hands.

These same patterns repeated themselves numerous times, and each time the defenders either stole the ball from her in the trap, or she fouled a player or dribbled the ball out of bounds. Danielle ignored the directions being shouted by Coach Miller and refused to pass the ball to her teammates.

For some reason, she returned to the same right side of the court, with the same two players blocking her from advancing toward the goal. Danielle and her team watched their lead dwindle and then disappear completely. Suddenly they were behind!

With Danielle in meltdown and unable to lead the team effectively, the coach took her out of the game and put her on the bench. She was incensed! If only she'd had a few more tries, she believed she could've beaten the defenders.

The game ended with Danielle's team losing. "It's Coach Miller's fault!" she declared as she slammed out of the gym. During the first half, she ran her game and they were winning. "The second half, the coach takes me out, and we lose!" she lamented. Danielle couldn't believe he had taken her out of the game.

That weekend, Danielle drove over to her grandpa's house, certain he'd let her vent about the loss. Danielle talked and talked about her coach. "He was mean. He was unfair. He took me out of the game!" The angry girl was convinced she could've turned the game around if only she'd had more opportunities to try.

Grandpa listened quietly and then smiled with an all-knowing look on his face. Finally, he said, "Let me ask you a question. As you were driving down the court the first half, what were you focused on?"

"Scoring," Danielle said haughtily.

"And in the second half, what were you focused on?"

"Well, getting past those freaking defenders!" she answered irritably.

Her grandfather smiled and said softly, "Danielle, you get what you focus on."

Danielle sat there, not knowing what to say. "What the hell did that mean?" she wondered.

He continued, "You get what you focus on. In the first half of the game, you were focused on scoring. As soon as you became fixated on the obstacle in your way, in this case the defenders, you could no longer see the goal, scoring. You took your eye off the goal, and focused on the obstacle. Guess what happened? You got more obstacles and they eventually led to defeat."

Danielle was confused. Her grandfather was talking about her focus, rather than blaming the coach. Sensing her feelings, he asked another question. "Why, after failing several times, didn't you change your focus back to scoring?"

"Well, because I was doing what had always worked!" said Danielle, frustrated.

"Yes, but they changed the game. They changed how they played you. Why did you remain focused on the defenders, and not refocus on scoring?"

Danielle was beginning to see his point, as much as she hated to admit it.

He continued, "This situation is a perfect metaphor for life. When things are working in our favor, God sometimes changes the game to help us grow into all that we are capable of becoming. The key to navigating life's curve balls is to remember that you get what you focus on. When the game changes, don't beat your head against the wall trying to do it the way you've always done it. Focus on your goal, and find another way."

Danielle's mouth fell open. In this particular game, when the defenders started to block her on the right hand side of front court, all she had to do was shift the ball from her right hand to her left and go to the other side of the court.

It wasn't any more complicated than that. She could have easily shifted the ball and dribbled down the left side of the court, or passed the ball to her teammates before the opponent set the trap on her. Yet she didn't see any of these options because she was focused on the obstacle, not the goal.

His words repeated in her head. "You get what you focus on. Focus on the goal, not the obstacle."

As he let Danielle absorb the message, he also wanted her to understand how broadly to apply its wisdom. "Do you know where I first learned this valuable lesson? I was a young man in a Wisconsin community hit hard by the Great Depression. I noticed that about 80 percent of the people in our town – well, their lives got worse as the depression wore on. But for the other 20 percent or so, even in those difficult times, their lives got better."

He added, "I was fascinated and wondered what the difference was between the 80 percent and the 20 percent. For the longest time, I couldn't find a difference. They came from similar backgrounds, some had jobs and some didn't, some had kids and some didn't. Some were single and others were married. Some went to church and others didn't. They were the same kind of people in the same situation, but some fared well while others didn't." He looked off to a different time and place, nodding.

"Finally I figured it out. During one of the worst times in our nation's history – a time that was incredibly scary – most people focused on their fear and anger. But those 20 percent, well those people...no matter what happened, they looked for the good. They focused on their goals, and how they could take advantage of the difficult circumstances and leverage them to good. That's when I realized that we have to be careful what we focus on, because that's what we get."

Grandpa reached over and gave Danielle a great big hug, the kind that only a grandpa can. "Danielle, life has already thrown you several obstacles and there will be more. Remain focused on what you want and be careful, because you will get what you focus on."
A few months later, Grandpa's advice returned not only to save Danielle, but also to transform the course of her life.

It was the end of her junior year and something unusual had happened. There'd been an armed robbery at a local restaurant and one of Danielle's friends, Pam, was held up at gunpoint. Pam and a coworker had been marched into the freezer before the robbers took off with the cash.

Danielle was worried and sought Pam out at school. When Pam saw Danielle, she pulled her aside and said, "Hey girl, I need to talk to you. I don't know how to tell you this, but I think one of the gunmen was your brother Jimmy. I couldn't see his face because he had a mask on, but I recognized his voice and he knew my name."

Danielle was stunned. Even though her brother was involved with drugs, she'd never seen him with a gun. Armed robbery?

Danielle thought about it all afternoon. Maybe Pam was right. Jimmy seemed to be flush with cash lately. She felt she had to do something. If he had really committed armed robbery, someone could have gotten hurt. So on the way home from school, she went by the police station to tell what she knew.

The officer asked a few questions about her brother. Then he sat her down in a chair and said, "Based on what you're telling me and the evidence we found at the restaurant, it's a strong possibility that your brother participated in this crime. However, because you're a minor, we need permission from your parents to take your statement."

Danielle drove home with incredible sadness in her heart. Although going to the police was the right thing to do, she couldn't believe her brother would participate in armed robbery. If it were true, he had to be held accountable for his actions.

She waited for her parents to come home. As her mom walked in the door, Danielle told her about her trip to the police station. Even though she didn't know exactly what to expect, she was unprepared for her mother's angry reaction.

As she finished explaining that the cops wanted her mom to sign a form so they could use Danielle's statement, her mother flew into a rage. "Why'd you do that?" she roared.

"Because someone could have gotten hurt," Danielle stammered, "And what Jimmy did was wrong."

Danielle's mother was livid. "You care more about your stupid friends than this family! I can't believe you did this to us!"

The day's drinking fueled her mom's rants. She continued to

throw out ugly and hurtful comments at Danielle...

- You are stupid
- You are terrible
- You only care about yourself
- You ain't no good

As Danielle listened to the poisonous words hurled at her, she felt caught between the part of herself that believed her mom's mean words, and the part that knew she had done the right thing and didn't deserve this tirade.

Danielle didn't know what to believe, but she knew it was a no-win situation and started to walk away. This time her mother followed her, not yet ready to quell the fight between them.

"Get back here!" She grabbed Danielle's face as she spewed obscenities at her daughter. "You didn't answer me. How could you do this?" she screamed.

"Because it was the right thing to do, Mom! Someone, including Jimmy, could have been killed!" she retorted.

As the words left her mouth, Danielle saw her mom's fist coming toward her face. As the fist connected with Danielle's jaw, the teenager's body flew across the room and landed against the wall. She was stunned and dazed.

Danielle touched her face, and wiped off the blood that was trickling down from where a ring had torn her skin. Every cell in her body called for her to get up and slug her mother as hard as she could. She'd never hit either parent before, but she was ready now. Seconds later, she started up off the floor. Fists ready and gritting her teeth, Danielle set her body to launch the attack. Immediately, her mother bent down in a perfect fighter's pose, waiting for Danielle to hit back and unleash the rage that had loomed silently for years.

As Danielle started toward her mom with a burning, shaking anger, a familiar voice inside her heart cried out: "You get what you focus on, Danielle. Focus on your future. This is another obstacle. You are better than this."

She knew it was Gramps. His gentle voice caused her to pause.

Danielle slowly took a step back, with every bit of effort she could muster. All of the anger, pain and hurt were begging to be unleashed in a way that would be irreversible. Astoundingly, she lowered her clenched fists and turned her attention away from her mother, looking upward and then closing her eyes. Knowing that her future rested on this very decision, she thought carefully about her next move. If she fought her mother, she would not stop. It would be a fight to the death. This was a defining moment in her life.

The choice became clear. She had to leave. It was her only hope of accomplishing her goal of building a better life. Danielle walked past her mother and into her room, hurriedly packing as many clothes as her gym bag would carry. As the girl walked out, she turned to her mother and said, "I don't deserve to be treated this way. I won't be back."

Danielle had no plan for how she would survive. But she knew there was something better out there and it was time to find it. From a payphone at the corner store, she called Gramps. She told him how his words had saved her that day, but it was like he already knew. He told her, "You can stay with me, honey. You made the right decision." For the rest of the year, he helped her put her life together so she could graduate high school. Every day he would ask, "Danielle, what are you focused on?"

"Graduation, Gramps!" she'd say.

"And then what?"

"College," Danielle would say.

"That's my girl," the elder wise man would say, his love showing for his beloved granddaughter.

Danielle vowed to never forget her grandpa's words and how they had led her out of a life of violence and eventually to college with a future filled with hope.

Although she believed in her own inner strength and no longer felt like a victim, she still carried a sense that there was more to do: mountains to climb, challenges to face.

As she packed her car to leave for college, opening a new phase in her life, she felt in control of her destiny for the first time. "You get what you focus on," she said as she hugged her grandfather goodbye and jumped into her car.

Silently, an angel gently pushed the young girl's car forward with a blessing and whispered into the old man's ear, "Well done."

SECTION TWO

TRANSFORMATION: Survivor Into Thriver

CHAPTER

8

SUCCESS IS A CHOICE

Choice: Who We Are is God's Gift to Us. Who We Become is Our Gift to God

Danielle hid the chemistry test under her literature textbook in embarrassment. The boldly marked "F" told her everything she already suspected; she was a failure and would never graduate college. She was "no good for nothing," like her mom had always told her.

So many of her mother's expressions repeated in her head, as if they had been tape-recorded. Danielle wanted to believe in her newly discovered capabilities, but sometimes, despite her best efforts, the hurtful words of the past haunted and eroded her confidence like rust erodes metal.

Occasionally, Danielle would receive support from her relatives, and subsequently, she would start to flourish. But when left unattended at an emotional crossroad, she would quickly lose hope. The tapes in her mind replayed mercilessly at the most critical junctures of her college career.

After barely eating a paltry lunch, the dejected college junior dragged into her favorite class, British Literature, still stinging from the failing grade in Chemistry. Anticipating a struggle with the subject matter, Danielle had waited as long as possible to take that class. Even though science had been her worst subject in high school, the Chemistry course was a graduation requirement.

Near the end of the British Literature class, her professor asked Danielle to come to her office. As the young girl dumped herself in the empty chair beside the desk, Dr. Carmichael, her favorite professor, asked, "What's wrong, Danielle? You don't seem yourself."

"I don't think I belong here. I can't do it. I can't graduate." Danielle said in defeat.

Her teacher said, "What? What are you talking about? How could you say that?"

Danielle lamented, "I can't do it anymore. I can't keep trying so hard when I know I will fail."

"Fail at what?" Dr. Carmichael asked. "You're on the Dean's List almost every semester!"

"Well, I need to pass Chemistry to graduate, and I can't do it." With those words of resignation, she pulled out her test with the failing grade clearly on it. "See? I can't do it. I won't graduate."

The kindly professor looked at the test and smiled. She had watched Danielle battle with confidence many times in the three years the young girl had been on campus. Each time Danielle faced a hurdle, she perceived it as a judgment about her own self-worth. Dr. Carmichael didn't know much about Danielle, but guessed she'd had a difficult life.

"Danielle, success is a choice." Dr. Carmichael stated matter-of-factly. "Every thought is a choice. You are choosing to believe you are a failure. It's your choice. As an adult, you get to decide whether or not you will succeed."

"But Chemistry is way different than my other courses. I've

always struggled with science. That's why I waited so long to take that course, and now that I am failing, I won't graduate."

"Danielle, I never said Chemistry wasn't hard, or that you wouldn't struggle. Remember how you struggled with accounting last year? And you wanted to quit back then, too. I believe you even told me math was one of your worst subjects and that you had always wrestled with it. How did you end up doing in that accounting class, Danielle?"

"Well, I had to work really hard. I studied more than most people, but I got lucky and ended up with a B+." She replied, missing the point.

"You did more than that. You had to face your fear, Danielle. And you decided that you would succeed, right?" The professor chided.

"I guess so, but I don't know what you mean by deciding that I would succeed. I worked hard and got lucky," Danielle said, with her lack of confidence in full force.

"Danielle, you're missing the point. Those thoughts in your head, those thoughts about being a failure and not being good enough: you're making all that up. You're choosing to believe that you will fail. It's your belief that's blocking your success," Dr. Carmichael said.

"Oh, so it's that simple? I decide I can pass Chemistry and poof, a magic elf takes my exams for me?" Danielle retorted, wearing her frustration outwardly.

"Danielle, stop it. You know it doesn't work that way. What I am talking about is deciding that you can do it before you even try. It's a choice. Success is a choice. You get to choose whether you will succeed, first in your mind, and then in your actions," the professor said.

"Maybe, but there's like this audiotape in my head that keeps telling me that I'm not smart enough," the girl admitted out loud.

"Well then, the question is whether or not you'll choose to

listen to that tape, or record a new one, isn't it? Now go and start changing your thoughts on the matter," Dr. Carmichael added.

"Ok. Thanks, Dr. Carmichael," Danielle said as she wearily dragged herself out of the building.

While walking across campus toward the library, she thought about the "voices" in her head, the ones who told her she was "stupid". She knew where they came from. Her mom's favorite expression always involved the word stupid. She'd say, "You're stupid," or "that's a stupid idea." Somewhere along the way, Danielle had internalized those words to mean she was stupid.

As she reflected upon her mom's words, she felt doubt returning. "Why do I think I am not worthy?" she wondered. "And, how is this affecting the way I approach my future?"

Instantly, her grandfather's voice popped into her head. "You get what you focus on, Danielle." It was almost like he was there in the library with her.

Of course! She was focusing on the recent failure and the negativity of her parents. It was true that she had failed, but now she was totally focused on failing.

"Success is a choice," she thought to herself. She let the words sink into her mind. Although they didn't feel comfortable, she knew she had to refocus on something other than failure.

The next morning, she went by Dr. Carmichael's office and found the professor grading papers.

"Hey, Dr. Carmichael, can I ask you a question?"

"Of course, Danielle. What's up?"

"Well, I get that if I focus on failing, I will fail. What I don't get is how I can choose success when it's clear from my first test grade that I am far from a success," the girl asked, perplexed.

"Danielle, you're right. What you must realize is that you get to pick what you focus on. You can choose to believe that you can succeed."

Danielle still looked puzzled.

"Danielle, I learned this phrase from a former college boyfriend who ran track. He always said, 'Success is a choice.' Even if he fared poorly in a race, he would focus solely on the races he had won before. He chose to believe he was a success, regardless of the outcome.

"It didn't mean that he didn't make modifications to techniques or learn from his mistakes, but he chose to believe he was a success first and foremost, and that's all he focused on. If he didn't make the decision in his mind first, his actions would be that of someone who didn't believe he could do it."

At long last the concept was becoming clear in Danielle's mind. She looked at Dr. Carmichael and smiled. "Ok, I think I get it. So, first I have to decide that I can pass Chemistry, and then I have to take the actions that match that decision."

"Yes! It sounds easy, but most people do not purposefully choose success. And here's another thing: not choosing is mediocrity by default," Dr. Carmichael added with a smile.

"Now I understand. I must choose to believe that I am a success before I even begin," Danielle said as she turned to leave the professor's office.

Danielle headed straight to her dorm, repeating "I choose to believe I can learn Chemistry" as she moved across campus. By the time she entered her small dorm room, the confidence she had felt in the professor's office had vanished. In its place were doubts and fears that operated almost as ghosts in her mind, stealing her self-confidence.

Danielle tapped herself on the head and proclaimed loudly to herself, "SUCCESS IS A CHOICE. I CAN DO THIS."

She continued, "OK. In order to pass this class, I will need help, so maybe I should find a tutor." As the words crossed her lips, she saw an advertisement in the school newspaper pinned to the bulletin board. A senior Chemistry major was looking for underclassmen who needed tutoring in Chemistry, Biology or Physics.

"No way," she exclaimed. "No freaking way!" She called the tutor, explained her predicament, and learned he would be available that afternoon to help her. Better yet, he agreed to lower his tutoring fee!

Three weeks later, Danielle took her second Chemistry exam. She knew when she left the room that she had at least passed the test, and for the first time since she entered college, she started to think about graduation. She could see it and feel it, walking down the aisle, graduating from college.

Two days later, she got her exam results and couldn't help but smile: B-. To further fuel her excitement, the professor wrote on the top, "'Great improvement!" She bolted out of the building toward her British Literature class in anticipation of sharing the news with Dr. Carmichael.

"Dr. Carmichael, I did it. I passed my Chemistry test, and I got a decent grade. Granted, I spent a great deal of time with the tutor preparing for the exam, but I did it."

"That's great Danielle. I knew you could do it. So, have you decided that you will indeed graduate, then?" the professor asked with a smile.

"Yeah, I decided. Besides, if I can pass Chemistry, I can do anything." Teasingly she added, "After all, it's my choice."

CHAPTER

9

YOU GET WHAT YOU GIVE

Give: Love is a Gift Only
When Given

For years, Gramps had been a fortress in the storm of Danielle's life. During her college years, she called him every other week, sharing fears and triumphs as he listened patiently. At the end of each call, he'd always say, "Hey, what are you focused on?" Danielle would respond, "Graduation," to which he always answered, "That's my girl."

Even after Danielle graduated college and her career took off, she continued to use her grandfather as a sounding board. He smiled as she constantly raised her goals. He was so proud of this little dynamo who refused to quit, despite the difficult challenges placed in front of her.

Over time, as she focused more and more on her career, Danielle called her grandfather less. However when something didn't work out the way she planned, like most people, she would inevitably let fear get the best of her and begin to focus on what wasn't working. At some point, she'd pick up the phone and call her grandfather, who predictably was there to tell her, "Hon, you get what you focus on." Danielle would always laugh and then turn her attention back to her goals, laughing at herself for losing sight of the most obvious of all of her lessons. It was funny how that happened; how she had to keep learning some of the most basic lessons over and over again.

In 1993, while serving as the director of marketing for a software company, Danielle got the phone call she dreaded. Gramps had passed away in his nursing home.

She flew home in tears, regretting that she hadn't called him in a month or so, and wishing she'd spent more time with him over the last year. But since he had entered the nursing home, it had been too draining for Danielle to see him that way.

Danielle met her parents and brothers at the nursing home, and the broken family came together temporarily in a unified team to pay tribute to a man who had been a rock in their family. Her parents, usually drunk and obnoxious, were unusually subdued. They were worried about Danielle, and even tried to comfort her, knowing how difficult this would be for their only daughter who was the apple of her grandfather's eye.

Slowly, Danielle walked into her grandfather's room and immediately saw the pictures, most of them of her, sitting on his dresser. As her mom went through his clothes, she motioned for Danielle to join her. In her hand was an envelope with Danielle's name on it. "Hon, it looks like he left this for you," her mom said.

Danielle took the envelope and walked out of the room in tears to find a private area to read it. She didn't want to share her pain with her family because regardless of their attempt to console her, they were still incapable of meeting basic emotional needs.

She opened the envelope, and in it was a handwritten note that said, "Danielle, I love you more than life itself. Your courage, desire and hard work are an inspiration. I don't have money to give you, but I've tried to leave you gifts along the way." Danielle's thoughts flashed to some of those gifts, and she smiled through her tears while reading on.

"The best gift I can give is the wisdom that was given to me." And then he had written a list of the little sayings he had shared with Danielle and her brothers throughout his life, pearls of wisdom that guided Danielle most every day.

"Know that I will always watch over you from heaven. I will always be here for you. Never doubt that. I will always live in your heart and your memories through some of the lessons that God asked me to pass along to you."

Danielle's heart was heavy and yet filled with love as she felt his presence surround her every breath. She glanced at the list of sayings, but noticed her favorite wasn't there: The one phrase that had gotten her through so many trying times. For a moment Danielle thought, "Maybe he didn't know how much it meant to me," as she felt the sadness of that thought, on top of the sadness of her loss.

Then, on the back of the letter, he had written, "What are you looking for? Ha ha. OK, I've got one more gift for you. Check my cigar box in the closet."

Danielle chuckled. "That's like him," she thought. "Always playing pranks."

About that time, Danielle's father came out of the room with a cigar box that had her name taped on the top. He said, "Danielle, he left this cigar box for you, too."

Danielle opened the box, and in it was a small jewelry box that contained her grandmother's wedding ring. Her grandmother died when she was young and although Danielle could hardly remember her, she knew Gramps loved her like there was no tomorrow.

Danielle opened the jewelry box and inside it was her grandmother's wedding ring with another note wrapped neatly around it. One side of the note read, "I leave you this gift from the soul mate I had on this earth so that no matter what happens, you will always remember that you are loved and cherished."

Danielle broke down. Gramps had said love moved in a circle and that's why wedding rings were symbols of love.

With tears streaming down her face, she turned the note over, and on the other side, it read in large letters, "Remember, you get what you focus on. Danielle, share this gift with others as I have with you. Because, not only do you get what you focus on..." and then in big letters...."YOU ALSO GET WHAT YOU GIVE."

Danielle made a promise right there to the presence that surrounded her in this very sad moment, a presence that she surely felt was her grandfather.

"Gramps, I will share this gift."

Somehow, someway, she would share his wisdom and pass along a gift that had gotten her through so many challenging times. She would keep the circle in motion.

CHAPTER
10

DON'T TRY TO RULE THE WORLD: TRANSFORM IT

Transformation: Thoughts Become Words, Words Become Actions and Actions Determine Character

It had been several years since Danielle's grandfather had died, and although she worked endless hours to support her career, there was an emptiness to her life. She pushed herself harder every day, never stopping to feel emotions, always driven to conquer the latest assignment or challenge tossed her way. It was almost as if that little-girl part of her who felt like "she wasn't good enough" had become engulfed by a career woman who tried to prove she was indeed good enough, by working ridiculous hours and trying to tame her world by brute force.

Her management responsibilities increased significantly due to her "get-it-done" personality and she was soon promoted to vice president over a large division. This division had been underperforming and she was asked to lead seven managers and more than 120 employees in the turnaround. She accepted the challenge as the next mountain to climb and soon had her new team at full attention.

Although she drove herself the hardest, she drove her team as well. Nothing was ever "good enough" and Danielle was never satisfied with accomplishments. Her expectations were unrealistic and frustrating. Her team of managers raised concerns, but Danielle dismissed them, referring to her management team as "cry-babies."

After an especially hard week when her entire department had worked overtime, Danielle ranted about the sales reports and said her team "wasn't doing enough to drive the turnaround." Had the economy been better, it's certain her entire team would have deserted the company, but most had no choice but to endure the constant berating. Despite their intense efforts, the turnaround was only mildly successful.

Up to this point, Danielle had been a rising star, attracting the attention of the C-suite officers who marveled at her success and determination. She felt like she had let them down. She felt like she had failed. All this did was spur her demanding style to new heights.

After a few months, she heard that the president, David Banner, would be visiting their division. David was an engaging leader who had inspired her on many occasions, and she looked to him for guidance as well as validation. She was embarrassed that their division's performance was so weak, and dreaded his visit for the first time in her entire career. In the past, she had cherished those moments when David singled her out for praise, both publicly and privately. She marveled at the way he could inspire people to new levels of performance. He was an eloquent speaker, and the larger the group, the more powerful he became.

"How would she face him?" she wondered. How would she be able to look him in the eye knowing that she had let him down? He was a person who had believed in her...

When David arrived, he immediately went to Danielle's office. He smiled as she feebly gave him updates on the initiatives underway to "improve things."

"That's not why I'm here, Danielle," he said. Instantly, Danielle stopped dead in her tracks. "I am going to be fired," she thought. "My career at this company is over."

David looked at her, and watched as panic drained all of the color out of her face. He had never understood why this amazingly intelligent woman was so unsure of herself.

"The division's performance is good enough for now," he said as Danielle waited for the guillotine to take off her head.

"It is?" she asked questioningly.

"Yes. I didn't come here to talk about the division. I came here to check on you," David said with obvious concern in his voice.

"Uh...well, I am fine, David," she lied.

"Really?" David inquired. "Are you really fine?"

"Yes, I am. But I can't seem to get my team to put in the effort to speed up this turnaround. They don't have what it takes."

"They don't? What do you think we should do, Danielle?" David asked slyly.

"Well, I was thinking about firing a few managers. That will get their attention, I think," Danielle said decisively.

"Really? Well, what have you tried so far?" David asked, already knowing that his rising star was missing an incredible leadership opportunity, choosing instead to burn out herself and her team.

As Danielle launched into a litany of programs and initiatives she had put in place, David listened intently. She labored over charts and graphs, and outlined the various strategies she had devised and implemented.

"And none of these are working?" David said.

With those words, Danielle slumped in her chair, feeling a lead balloon of defeat press its full weight against her. She realized that she might indeed be fired, yet she couldn't bring herself to admit that frankly, she didn't know what to do.

As David inquired and poked and prodded, Danielle became more and more deflated. Finally, she said flatly, "David, I don't know what to do."

"Ah," he said. "Good. Great leaders know what they don't know."

"What?" Danielle said, confused and bewildered.

"Well, most people don't know what they don't know. Yet, most executives try to fake it, never admitting they don't know how to fix something. If you think you know how to fix a problem, you're bound to overlook real solutions. I find that when executives really don't know what to do, they do one of two things. Some belittle every idea presented to them, believing if they aren't smart enough to solve the problem, no one else is either. Others focus on all of the problems except the core issues. And both of these strategies have dire consequences."

Danielle sat there quietly, absorbing everything David was saying.

"Real leaders know what they don't know and admit it." David said almost in a whisper, waiting for Danielle to admit what they both knew was obvious.

"OK, David, I don't know how to turn this division around. That's the truth," Danielle said with a slight tremble in her voice.

"Good, now we're on to something!" David exclaimed gleefully.

"What does your management team think we should do?" he asked, already knowing the answer.

"They haven't offered any real solutions, only excuses," Danielle replied, her face getting hotter.

"Really? A group of people with twice your experience doesn't have any suggestions?" David asked. "Tell me the truth, Danielle, have you listened to them?"

"Well, uh, yeah, but they make excuses. I am tired of it, David. I want performance," Danielle stated loudly.

"Performance, huh?"

"Yes, damn it!" Danielle's frustration returned at the thought of her management team's excuses. She worked hard and sacrificed every day, trying to find the solutions, so why couldn't they?

David waited for Danielle to regain her composure.

"Danielle, when I was a young executive, I made a couple of critical mistakes, and I think you're making the same ones," David said softly, trying to ease his budding star into this teachable moment.

"Ok, what mistakes am I making?" Danielle asked, trying to contain her fear of being fired.

"Well, my mentor told me this. 'Don't try to rule the world, transform it.' I think you're so busy trying to drive and rule and act like a leader that you're missing one of the basic tenants of transformation. Transformation occurs when people share a common vision and are motivated to passionately work toward that vision."

Danielle sat there quietly, as memory flashes of her overbearing style came to mind. Scenes where she had cut people off, snapped at them, and dismissed their ideas. They all came rushing toward her, taking the air out of her lungs briefly.

David continued, "Have you worked with them to build a vision for what you want to accomplish? Have you encouraged their ideas and rewarded their sacrifices?"

"Well, uh..." Danielle stammered.

"Danielle, you can't rule the world. You can't rule your management team, even though they report to you. You have to inspire them to want to transform themselves, their departments and this division. Not because they have to, but because they want to!" David said, his eyes sparkling with a fiery passion that was intoxicating to Danielle.

"Know what you don't know. You don't know what to do, right?" David asked, knowing he had his star pupil right in the midst of a personal transformation.

"Yes, that's true," Danielle said flatly.

"Perfect. The first step is to admit that to your management team," David said as he watched shock wash over Danielle's face.

He smiled, "And, you also have to admit that you've been unreasonable, demanding and a ruthless leader. Tell them the truth. If you want their respect, tell them the truth. It will get their attention faster than any program you can implement."

"You want me to do what?" Danielle asked in complete disbelief.

"Tell them the truth. Then apologize. Give them a three-day weekend off, and encourage them to rest. Let them know that when they return, you will indeed listen to them, individually and as a group. Tell them the only way we can turn around this division is if they come up with the best ideas. Tell them you want their ideas, because you don't know how to fix this, and they have more experience than you do. Tell them the truth," David said again for effect.

"But they won't respect me, David," Danielle said, petrified.

"Yes, they will. People want to be led. And, they want to be led by someone who will tell them the truth. I know it sounds crazy, but it will work. The truth is – and you're not going to like this – they already know you don't know what to do, Danielle. Your best shot of winning their respect is to admit the truth, and then encourage them to partner with you to turn this around."

David waited a moment for that painful truth to be absorbed into the young woman's mind. "And people don't want to be told what to do. What they want is for their leader to isolate and clarify problems. Then, they want to be given the latitude to transform the problems. Lastly, they want a leader who will give them credit and who will remove obstacles that are getting in the way of solving their problems. What you perceive as excuses, they perceive as obstacles. Remove a few of their obstacles and you'll fuel their fire," David added.

As he finished, David looked up and saw Danielle feverishly writing. Her anguish had been replaced with a tinge of excitement.

"OK, so the first thing I do is call a meeting with the management team. I open the meeting and say, 'Guys, I need to tell you the truth. As hard as we've worked, we have not turned around this division. Frankly, I don't know what to do. I do know this: each of your departments has worked hard, and I have been too demanding. I also haven't listened to your ideas. What I'd like to do is to give each of you, and all of your teams, a three-day weekend so we can rest. When we return Monday, let's tackle the solutions together. You have my commitment that I will shut up and listen.' Something like that, right David?" Danielle asked, checking to make sure she understood.

"Danielle, that's perfect! Now, one other thing. Although they'll be glad that you're admitting the obvious, and even happier to have some time off, don't expect them to come in transformed on Monday. Most will be suspicious that when they return, you will still be your demanding self. Most will not be prepared with ideas, because they won't believe you will actually listen. You're going to have to find a way to prove to them that you do indeed mean to listen."

"OK, David. I can do that!" Danielle said with enthusiasm.

As David turned to leave, he put his hand on her arm and said, "Danielle, I am proud of you. Don't try to rule the world, transform it." And he walked away with a slight bounce in his step, believing even more in her.

The next day, Danielle had the meeting with her management team, and on Monday, as David had predicted, they returned with no solutions and faces filled with anxiety, certain that at any moment, the other shoe would drop and the evil witch would return.

Instead, what they found was a list of challenges and barriers for each of their departments. Danielle met with them individually and said something to the effect: "I've identified what I believe are the top three challenges in your department. I tried to make them as clear as I could, but I need you to verify that I captured them correctly. You can solve the challenges any way you want; just review your suggestions with me before you implement them. More importantly, here are the top three barriers I see, barriers that you've told me are preventing you from being successful. I commit that while you are working on coming up with solutions, I will work at removing the barriers."

The management team was dumbfounded. They shot each other glances, like "is this for real?" As Danielle honored her promise and started removing barriers for them, their energy and enthusiasm shifted. As she praised their ideas and solutions, their intensity grew. As she rewarded their successes, they indeed transformed.

Three months later, results were strong. The division was slowly but surely climbing out of its last-place spot on the company roster.

Shortly after receiving a call from David thanking her for doing such a great job and encouraging her to take a little time off to celebrate, Danielle took her first vacation in years. She went to her favorite beach with a few friends.

As she sat looking at the bright-blue sky, she listened to the powerful waves as they rushed ashore. She wondered about the ocean's ability to transform. She was reminded of Michelle Cooper, and how Michelle had told her real power was more like water than a hammer. She wanted to lead that way, like the ocean. Transforming, but not overpowering. She thought about how good it felt to lead her team. She wondered if she would ever be as smart as David, and if she would ever be able to lead people the way he did.

CHAPTER
11

YOU ACT OUT WHAT YOU BELIEVE ABOUT YOURSELF

Belief: Life Mirrors
Our Thoughts

Having found a much more effective leadership style thanks to David's mentoring, Danielle was lured away from the software company where she had her professional roots, to become president of an Internet subsidiary at age 34. It was an unexpected twist in her career. She quickly motivated her new team and then led the new company to record-setting performance. As a result, she was generously rewarded with stock options as the company navigated its Initial Public Stock Offering in the late 90s. The Internet was the place to be, and everything seemed to line up perfectly. Although she missed David's mentoring, this was truly a dream job and she put everything she had into it.

Danielle used her career to give her the elusive self-value that had escaped her during childhood. Consequently, she sacrificed her personal life and even her health. Danielle steadily gained weight while fixating on the professional challenges placed before her. When her scale tipped over 200 pounds, she knew she was fat. Danielle felt ashamed when she went clothes-shopping and was forced to buy a larger size. At 5'4", she soon moved from the petite section of the department store where the suits capped at size 14 to the "Large

Woman" section. She was utterly embarrassed. "Large Woman" professional attire looked frumpy and unattractive.

It was January 1, 1999 and like many who set New Year's resolutions, Danielle set a goal to lose 25 pounds in the next six months. She joined her local gym and put together a meal plan to reduce her calorie intake to less than 1800 calories per day. She did well the first two weeks, but by the end of January, Danielle couldn't seem to resist the urge to grab a bag of potato chips between meals, and soon dropped the workout routine all together. By March, she had gained an additional five pounds and was even more depressed. On top of the weight gain, Danielle's health was compromised due to the constant stress placed on her body by her addiction to work. She didn't know what to do.

As with everything in Danielle's life, fate soon intervened and she was invited to two workshops by two different friends. The combination of these events opened a transitional door Danielle wanted to enter, albeit grudgingly. Over the course of a few months, Danielle participated in a workshop with John Milton Fogg and Iyanla Vanzant, two very different authors who happened to mention the EXACT same thing in their workshops. "We act out what we believe about ourselves," they each said. "Our life is a mirror of our beliefs about ourselves." They had Danielle's attention from the moment those words left their lips.

Iyanla said, "Somewhere in our first eight to ten years of life, we make decisions about ourselves. We decide, as children, whether or not we are 'good enough' or 'pretty enough' and then we spend the rest of our lives acting out those beliefs." Both speakers encouraged participants to write down their beliefs, or more accurately, to write down the "thoughts" that rummaged around their unconscious minds. To write down the things that they told themselves were true about "who they were."

During Iyanla's workshop, she brought an overweight participant up on the stage and helped the young man identify the beliefs he held that kept him imprisoned in his unfit body. As Danielle watched this young man wrestle with his own belief patterns, and then later connect those beliefs to his unhealthy eating habits, she knew she had found a key to unlock her own misery.

That night, she sat in her favorite chair and let herself write, for the first time ever, the horrid thoughts that bounced around her mind. Things she told herself when she made a mistake, or when she looked in the mirror and saw her own reflection staring back at her.

"I am fat."

"I am stupid."

"I am not good enough."

The words flowed out effortlessly onto her paper, and she could hear the phrases echoing in the recesses of her mind.

Tears softly welled up as she wrote the phrases on the page, gently pulling the terrible thoughts from the roots of her unconscious into her conscious mind. "Oh my God," she prayed. "How can I actually think these things about myself? I actually believe that I am not good enough. No wonder I treat myself so poorly!"

In the workshop, Iyanla talked about moving from being a victim to a survivor and that those who were doing the work to improve themselves – rather than blaming others – could claim that they were survivors. She also said that to move from being a survivor to a 'thriver' required more than "doing the work". It required healing old wounds.

Although Danielle couldn't comprehend what it would feel like to "thrive," she was tired of barely surviving. She was tired of putting herself last, and tired of feeling responsible for everything. Maybe this would work. After all, these beliefs were nothing more than chains to her past.

So she sat back and took a deep breath. What was the "cause" of these beliefs that she had about herself? For so many years, Danielle had pushed away childhood memories, in essence shutting out every memory, even the good ones. And, for the most part, shutting down every single emotion available to her.

"I am stupid." That one was easy. It was her mom's favorite expression, and she recalled how she had to fight that belief in college. She remembered how her professors helped her see that she was indeed smart. She recalled how she had to use her grades to remind herself that she was not stupid. She surmised that maybe that belief had been changed because her intelligence was the only thing she could count on, other than her willingness to work hard.

"I am fat." She let herself drift back to memories of how her father had commented on her naked body and told her to watch what she was eating so she wouldn't get fat. "Men don't like fat girls," he said.

She shuddered as his words replayed in her mind. Tears were flowing a little more quickly now, unlocking years of grief that felt like chains wrapped around her entire body. She instinctively knew this belief was seared deep in her mind, and because of the abuse it was not only difficult to comprehend, but would be even harder to heal. "That's going to take some time," she said to herself. Then she took a breath and relaxed, letting her mind drift to the next statement that stared at her like a tattered old coat that had long outlived its use, but still hung in the closet because its existence provided a familiar comfort.

"I am not good enough." Wow, she could think of hundreds of times that her parents had insinuated that! "How can I pick one?" she wondered out loud. Danielle closed her eyes and let her mind wander.

Like Iyanla had encouraged the overweight participant on the stage earlier that night, she encouraged herself to remember. She allowed herself to feel the pain. She said, "I am not good enough," and allowed herself to dwell in the feelings of being unworthy. Slowly her mind drifted back to a time when she was about six years old. It played out in her mind like a scene from a movie and she soon picked up her pen and wrote down the experience.

"I am about six, and it's raining outside. I feel cold and wet and all I can think about is getting home to the warm house. As I approach my house, I can tell no one is home, but I anxiously turn the door handle because I never know what to expect in my house."

Danielle stopped writing and underlined, "I never know what to expect in my house."

She continued, "I am so cold, and my clothes are wet. I want Mom to hold me. I want her to make me feel better."

Danielle stopped again and underlined the words, "I want to be held." She could feel the simple childlike desire of wanting to be held. Tears rolled down her cheeks as she continued replaying the scene and writing the words as they were released from the corners of her unconscious mind where they had been locked away for years.

"I am afraid that if I go into my room no one will check on me, and I will be alone. I look around and wonder where I can go so that someone will find me and take care of me. I need to get warm because it's so cold and wet. I look down the hall and see the furnace and decide that I will lie in front of the furnace to get warm. That way when Mom comes home she will see me. Then she'll pick me up and take care of me."

Danielle stopped writing. She could feel her body aching as if she were cold and wet and lying in front of a furnace without a blanket. She knew she was about to unearth an important discovery and moved forward with great trepidation.

"After a while, I hear Mom's car. I am so excited because finally, she will come and take care of me. She tosses her purse on the table and walks toward me. I put on my best 'possum' face, pretending to be asleep, all curled up in a ball. As Mom approaches she says, 'What are you doing there?' in an angry tone.

"In my best child's voice I say, 'I don't...feel...well.' And then Mom kicks me in the stomach and says, 'Well then get up and go to bed!'"

Danielle closed her notebook and sobbed. She could not stop the memory as she recalled this little six-year-old child lifting her tired, wet body off the floor, her stomach throbbing from where her mom had kicked her. She felt her own stomach ache from a hole inside her that was formed almost 30 years ago. As hard as it was, and as much as she wanted to turn off this memory, she followed the little girl to her bedroom.

Holding back a river of tears, she continued to write, "I am in my bed, and am trying to get warm by putting the covers around me. I lie there and think to myself. 'I am worthless. My Mom doesn't love me,' and with that, I drift off to sleep, the image and memory searing itself into my mind."

Danielle stopped journaling and allowed herself to weep, rocking back and forth. She wanted to throw up. Her stomach hurt so badly, yet there was relief mixed in with the pain.

Iyanla told the guy on stage that in many cases we have to "re-parent" ourselves using imagery of our "little child." So, she imagined her mom coming into her room and holding her, only it wasn't her mom. It was Danielle, as an adult, holding her little child and comforting her. She told her that she was indeed good enough and she loved her immensely. She then thought about her grandfather and how he would have responded if he had been the one to find her that day. She focused all of her energy on him and remembered how he loved her.

Soon, her tears subsided and she realized a belief had been formed that day; a belief that she wasn't good enough. This belief was reinforced over the years as her parents abused her. Then to compound the abuse, even worse still, she continued to "act out the belief" by abusing herself as an adult.

With this realization, came a mixture of relief and disappointment. Relief that she understood what was going on and disappointment that she let it happen.

Next, she made a list of the many ways she "proved to herself that she wasn't good enough." The list included: working too many hours, not taking a vacation, eating unhealthy foods, making bad relationship choices, being critical of her every waking moment and more. By the time she finished, it was after midnight and the list was more than a page long.

"This has to change," Danielle said as she tucked away her notebook and crawled into bed. As soon as she woke the next morning, she picked up the phone and called her insurance company's hotline to find an outpatient therapy center to get help. When she called the center, they told her she would have to take at least one day a week off work for eight weeks to complete the program.

At first, she panicked. There was no way she could do that with her current schedule. Then, she reminded herself that she had to put herself first in order to heal. So she sat down and wrote two letters. The first was a resignation letter and the second was a request for 12 days off over the next eight weeks "for personal reasons." Danielle wasn't sure if the chairman and CEO would grant the time off but she was prepared, if need be, to resign entirely.

Although she'd hardly taken any personal time since college graduation, she knew everything had to change if she was going to survive, much less thrive.

On her way to work, she called the CEO's secretary and explained that there was an emergency and she needed to meet with him as soon as possible.

She hung up the phone and gripped the steering wheel,

fighting off an impending sense of panic. The dread was followed by waves of incredible sadness at what she had done to herself. "I can't believe that I've treated myself this way." With resolve, she pressed the car onward and turned into the parking lot, carefully exiting the car and slowly heading into the building. She knew her life was about to take a turn, although she didn't know in what direction.

One thing she did know, which she repeated to herself as she walked into the CEO's office, "This time, I come first."

CHAPTER 12

SUCCEED ON PURPOSE

Grace: We Always Get
What We Need, Not What
We Want

Not only was Danielle successful in getting the time off and starting intense therapy, but slowly she lost weight and began to restore her health. She ushered in the new millennium feeling like a different person. Although she still worked a lot, for the first time ever, her life had a semblance of balance.

When the crushing blow of September 11, 2001 occurred, however, Danielle realized there was still something amiss. She needed to do more to put her life in perspective. She desperately wanted to work through the nagging sense that she wasn't where she was supposed to be.

So on September 14, Danielle resigned from her position as president of the Internet company. With no idea what she would do or where she would go, she focused on the one thing she did know: it was time for an extended break and everything else would work itself out.

Fortunately, she had the financial means to make such a risky move, although the thought of burning through her nest egg was terrifying. At the same time, she knew there wasn't a choice. So she packed it in, continued the intense therapy, enrolled in an Executive MBA program to enhance her professional skills, and began to search for a deeper sense of meaning in her career. She hired a business coach, read every book she could find on charting new professional pathways, and took several workshops on "life plans."

During one of these workshops, the participants did an exercise to find their "Life Mission Statement." She walked away from the workshop with a personal mission statement that read, "To inspire people to achieve their highest potential." Although Danielle didn't know what to do with it, she knew it was important and wrote out the statement on an index card and placed it in a drawer next to her bed.

A few months later, still unemployed and unsure what to do next, she heard a pastor at her local church make a comment about "succeeding on purpose." Danielle loved the statement, and thought about how she had always done things deliberately. It was one of the characteristics she valued most about herself.

She imagined how companies might benefit from a consultant who helped them "succeed on purpose," so she decided to form a training and consulting enterprise that would help companies be deliberate about success -- to plan it and execute. It was late 2002 when she launched Succeed on Purpose, Inc. and started the process of building the training and consulting company while completing her MBA program.

Using her network of contacts, she quickly picked up clients and helped with everything from marketing programs to strategic plans. Within a year she had replaced her executive salary, but for some reason it still felt like something was missing. She toyed with returning to a corporate position. As she and her business coach explored options, it became clear that Danielle was hungry to lead a team, and believed that she couldn't do that as an entrepreneur.

Together with her coach, she devised a strategy to take her

company to the next level. She built a business plan to hire and train employees to deliver the services she offered. Danielle was excited because she could inspire employees and help them become great consultants. She rebranded the company TotalMark, Inc., and focused its services on marketing consulting because that had become the largest portion of profits. Although she liked the name "Succeed on Purpose", it didn't sound like a world-class consulting firm.

In the summer of 2004, TotalMark launched. As with any start-up, Danielle invested a significant amount of time, energy and money to get the business up and functional. By the end of 2005, her firm was profitable and had 10 employees.

There was, however, one big problem. Danielle was now working 60-70 hours a week, overseeing every project and wearing multiple hats. A year later, TotalMark had 25 employees and although quite profitable, things were worse. Danielle was now working almost 80 hours per week. 2007 brought more growth and more stress.

Danielle found herself irritable, demanding and miserable. Her staff no longer enjoyed the coaching and avoided her almost completely. Also predictably, her weight had again burgeoned to more than 200 pounds and her personal life was again in shambles.

"I don't get it!" she said one day to her coach. "I thought that if I built my own company, I would be happy. Why is this happening to me?" she wondered resentfully.

Her coach did her best to explain that having a business was tough, and that although she had control, with more employees and more customers there was more stress. "Danielle, why don't you scale your business back?" her coach asked.

"I can't do that!" Danielle snapped. "We have a plan to hit. I want to expand into another city and maybe even acquire a company."

"If you continue to grow at this pace, you're only going to make matters worse," her coach argued. "Why don't you hire someone to run the company so you can take some time off?"

Danielle liked that idea, so she found a managing partner to run the firm. Although this move added stability to the firm, Danielle still had a nagging sense that something wasn't right.

Danielle's coach and counselor were both at a loss. "Danielle, you've built a successful company, you have less responsibility and you're making good money. Why aren't you happy?" they all asked incredulously.

Although Danielle tackled this plaguing question with the same zeal as everything else, she had no answer. She wasn't happy.

"Maybe I'll never be happy," she wondered out loud with her advisors. Once again, that ever-elusive sense that she didn't belong engulfed her. "I'm 41 years old, and no matter what I do, I can't be happy," she groused. She began to doubt herself, her coaches and her professional ability.

She didn't know what to do. Even though she was an excellent marketing strategist and her customers loved her, she absolutely hated what she was doing. At the same time, there didn't seem to be a way out. By now, the firm had almost 40 consultants, all of whom were dedicated to the success of the firm.

In the spring of 2008, a small door opened. As she was in the process of evaluating the purchase of a small company in Atlanta to expand her own firm, she did an economic analysis and discovered that a major market correction was coming in the next year that would change the business landscape completely.

It wasn't the right time to buy a company, so she called off the deal. Just as quickly as she pulled the plug, the holding company that owned the firm made Danielle a counteroffer. The chairman said, "Danielle, you have one thing of tremendous value to us: your Return on Investment (ROI) Tool."

Danielle knew he was right. To extend their services, her firm had built one of the first marketing ROI tools. She also knew that a consulting company would not make it through a major market correction if it lasted as long as economists were predicting this recession to last. Her employees would lose their jobs, and she might lose all of her investment in TotalMark. She also understood that her employees would stand a better chance of survival if they were in large corporations. She believed her customers would grab them quickly if given the chance. Better yet, it would give Danielle the "out" she so desperately wanted.

"OK, make me a deal," she said. Although the chairman had no idea how ready Danielle was to get rid of her business, within a month a deal was done and the holding company was thrilled to acquire the ROI tool.

Just as easily as throwing out the trash, she discarded the previous seven years spent building TotalMark. Although her employees were shocked that Danielle was quitting, they didn't realize it was a blessing for all, as they would be much better off working in large, stable companies when the crash hit.

Everything happened quickly and deliberately. With no clue how to find that elusive happiness on her own, Danielle took a position as the chief marketing officer for a multinational company that had been one of her favorite customers. "At least I will work normal hours and not have the stress of doing something I hate," she thought to herself.

As the moving company transferred the last pieces of furniture from her business office, a small piece of paper fell on the floor from her desk drawer. Danielle glanced at it, realizing quickly that it was nothing more than the old personal mission statement she had written before forming her original training and consulting company, Succeed on Purpose. She threw it away in disgust, much like she did all of the TotalMark memorabilia. But as she turned to lock the door to her office for the last time, something prompted her to pick up the piece of paper from the trash. She stuffed it in her pocket.

"Whatever," she said as she locked the door and carried the last box to her car. On the outside, it appeared as if a door was closing. However, to an angel perched above Danielle's office, it was the beginning of a magnificent transformation that would alter the lives of thousands of people... just as God had planned.

FORGIVENESS IS A BLESSING

Forgiveness Is a Blessing
When Freely Given

Danielle had only been on her new job a few months when a panicked call came in from her mom one Monday morning. "Danielle, your dad isn't doing well. He's in the hospital, and we're not sure he'll make it through the week. Can you come home...um...right now?"

"Sure, Mom. I'll jump on a plane as soon as I can," Danielle responded.

"Fine. Your brothers are on their way too. Please hurry."

Danielle hung up the phone and sat motionless. She could feel an indistinct emotion stirring in her chest, but couldn't identify what it was exactly. Brushing it aside, she began the task of clearing her calendar and securing a plane ticket.

Before leaving, she walked over to her secretary's office and explained, "Kris, I'm leaving now. I plan on coming back in a few days once the situation is assessed," she said clinically.

Kris hugged Danielle and slipped a card to her that all of

the employees had quickly and quietly assembled. It was filled with well wishes and loving thoughts. As Danielle tucked the card in her briefcase, she thought about how much she enjoyed this team and her new job. She believed she was helping people, and that made her happy. To have their support was an immeasurable gift. "Thanks, Kris," she said as she headed for the door.

While rushing to pack a small bag, Danielle let her mind wander to the last trip home for her parent's 50th wedding anniversary about three months ago. Although a happy occasion, she could tell her father wasn't well. It was difficult to assess either parent's health since they both continued to drink despite their age, but Danielle distinctly recalled he had an unusual grayish color to his face.

Although she didn't return to her parents' home frequently, the tremendous amount of therapy over the last 10 years left her relatively prepared for this moment. With the singular goal of growing from childhood pain, and at the same time not being chained to the memories, Danielle forgave her parents willingly and made peace with the past. It took much longer to forgive her father because of the sexual abuse which had robbed her of innocence and the ability to trust. Regardless, she had completely forgiven him.

When the plane touched down, Danielle rushed to get her luggage and the rental car. It was late afternoon and she quickly made the one-hour trip down the familiar highway toward her parents' home. As she was driving, her mind drifted back to thoughts of her childhood. She was overcome by a tightening in her chest and a tremendous feeling of loss and sadness. Danielle did not want to focus on random emotions right now, and was irritated that she could not easily dismiss this feeling. She took a deep breath and reminded herself of all the work she had done over the years. She reflected on how prepared she felt for this moment, and how proud she was of the healing that had occurred. She hoped her dad was still lucid when she arrived so they could say their goodbyes.

When Danielle pulled into the hospital parking lot, she prepared herself for the worst. Reaching the ICU floor, she immediately saw her younger brother Mark weeping on his wife's shoulder. She tentatively walked over to him, fearing she hadn't made it in time.

"Mark, you OK?"

"No, not really. I can't stand to see him like this," Mark said, as Danielle breathed a sigh of relief.

"Can I go in?" she asked.

"Of course. He's in room 506," Mark said, pointing down the hall.

Danielle turned and headed in the direction he had pointed. As she entered, she saw her mom sitting on the bed talking to her dad. "Hey Mom. I'm here," Danielle said softly.

"Hi hon. He is awake, but doesn't feel well. The doctor said the cancer returned,"

"Hey Dad, I came all this way to visit you and you're not even getting out of bed?" Danielle said trying to lighten the heaviness that hung over the room.

Her dad smiled slowly and lifted his hand in a weak attempt at a wave. Her mom added, "We've had time with him all day, so why don't the two of you catch up?"

"Sure, that would be great," Danielle said.

As her mom walked away, Danielle prepared herself for a conversation she'd rehearsed for years. She had imagined this moment a thousand times. Her dad on his death bed, asking for forgiveness and telling her how much he loved his only daughter.

Danielle grabbed his hand and gave him a peck on the forehead.

He asked her how she liked her new job, and Danielle spent the next 10 minutes or so describing the company she worked for, and how she felt like she was making a difference. He listened and nodded occasionally, but Danielle could tell he was getting tired, so she changed the subject to a more important matter.

"Dad, I want you to know that I will take care of Mom," she offered.

Her Dad replied, "I know you will. Plus your brother lives next door and he'll look after her too."

Danielle pushed further, "Dad, I want you to know that I love you very much."

"I know you do. I love you, too." He said, and then looked away wistfully.

"Dad, are you afraid to die?" Danielle asked straightforwardly.

"No, Hon, I've made peace with God," her dad said and then started to look a little sleepy.

"OK Dad, I'll let you get some sleep." She hugged him and then turned to leave, wondering if this would be as much as she'd get from him. "At least he's good with God, especially considering the anger that consumed most of his life," she thought to herself as she left the room.

Danielle talked to the rest of the family and made plans to meet the next morning. She returned to her hotel room and thought about the exchange. As much as she hated to admit it, she had always hoped – expected even – that her father would apologize. Even though she had forgiven him, it was the least he could do.

The next day was spent at the hospital reassuring her mom

that everything would be OK and checking in with the doctors about his prognosis. He had terminal cancer. Although they might let him go home, he would be in hospice care and probably would die in the next few weeks, if not sooner.

Realizing there wasn't much else she could do, and wanting to remove herself from the disappointment of the last exchange with her father, she explained that she needed to return to Dallas for work. She assured everyone that she'd come back that weekend and help get hospice set up.

"Sure, Danielle. I know you have to get back. I am glad you got here to say goodbye," her mom offered. Danielle hugged both parents and then her brothers and slipped out the hospital door.

Driving back to the airport, she felt a familiar emptiness associated with her father. "Well, that didn't go how I expected," she thought to herself.

When she returned to work Wednesday, her team was shocked. "What are you doing here?" Bill, the director of product marketing, exclaimed.

"Well, there's not much I can do, and I'll go back this weekend when they take him home and bring in hospice."

"What? You shouldn't be here. I can't even imagine what you're going through," Bill said sympathetically.

"Thanks, Bill, but I really am OK. I wasn't that close to my father and well, let's just say we've had an odd relationship."

"Ok, but still, it's got to be hard."

Danielle thanked him for his concern and left, wondering if maybe she should be feeling something more. Admittedly, she did have this nagging sentiment she couldn't quite explain. It was heavy.

On rare occasions, it would clutch at her heart and wash her in waves of unspoken sorrow. Those moments were fleeting, however, and Danielle did not commit herself to deciphering its meaning. After all, it was not as if she and her father had a close relationship.

Next, she made her flight arrangements for Friday night so she could spend the weekend with her family. Still sensing something amiss, she called her therapist and requested an appointment for Friday afternoon.

Friday mid-morning, her mom called and said, "Danielle, we brought him home early this morning. He said he wants to die at home. You need to get back now. I don't think he'll make it through the night."

"I'm on my way, Mom. The plane gets in at 10 tonight and I'll be at the house before midnight. Don't worry, I'll be there."

Even though she tried to reassure her mom, Danielle had a sick feeling in the pit of her stomach. She struggled to eat lunch and called to check on the availability of an earlier flight before leaving for her therapy session. There was a flight at 5 p.m. and she put her name on the standby list.

With her stomach twisted in knots, she slumped into the therapist's chair and unloaded. Susan listened patiently and then said, "Let me see if I understand. The father who abused you is dying. We've worked for years on forgiveness and healing. During that time you not only forgave your father and healed your wounds, but you also secretly believed that before your father died, he would ask you to forgive him? Did I get that right?"

"Yes, basically that's right, Susan," Danielle said tentatively.

"OK. Well, Danielle, given the emotional state you're in, I am not going to beat around the bush. I'm going to give it to you straight, OK?"

"Okaaayyy," Danielle said warily.

And then Susan said, "First, you are grieving, my dear. I realize this is a new emotion for you, but you are grieving."

Danielle was puzzled. "Grieving? Grieving what?"

"Yes. You may not be grieving the death of your father, because that would require you to have had a relationship with him, but you are certainly grieving the loss of never being able to have a relationship with him."

Carefully watching her patient's reaction, Susan added, "When we have estranged parents, there is a part of us – that little child part – who secretly hopes one day to have a magical parent-child relationship like the one about which we have always dreamed. When that estranged parent dies, we grieve the loss of the dream, as opposed to the loss of the relationship."

Danielle was stunned. Grieving the loss of what could never be? How profoundly accurate and acutely painful.

"You are right, Susan. That's exactly right. I know that I'll never have that relationship with him. It's compounded by the fact that he didn't apologize. I thought that maybe he would apologize, and for a brief second we'd have a father-daughter relationship," Danielle added.

"Good, now that we got that out of the way, there's more." Susan added.

"More?" Danielle asked hesitantly.

"Yes. Take a breath, Danielle," Susan said.

"You are waiting for your father to apologize and to ask for forgiveness, which in all of the years you've known him, he has never done. In fact, he's clearly demonstrated he is incapable of that very thing. So, you are expecting him to do something, on his death bed, of which he is incapable."

She paused for a second and then added, "Danielle, what you need to do is give him forgiveness! Not forgive him, but let him know you forgive him. The greatest gift you can give a person who has wounded you is to make sure that person does not die carrying regrets. Your father doesn't know how to ask for your forgiveness. So you're going to have to give it to him as a gift."

"Oh my God!" Danielle shrieked. "You're right!" As the awareness of this oversight came over her, she realized that she might not make it home in time to tell her father she forgave him. "Susan, I have to go right now. I've got to try to make it in time. Thank you so much."

She sprinted out of the office and headed for the airport. She was able to make it on the 5 p.m. flight to Tampa. She ran to the car-rental counter, picked up her car and drove like an Indy race car driver, praying to God that her dad would not die before she could tell him what he needed to hear – what she needed to tell him.

She dashed into the house. The entire family was in her father's room and the hospice nurse was on the couch. She looked at the nurse, inquiring with her facial expression. The nurse smiled and said, "He's waiting for you. He asked where you were. Your mom said he didn't want to leave without saying goodbye."

Danielle gulped, took a breath and wiped the lone tear from her face. She walked into the room and her mother got up out of the chair so she could sit next to her dad.

"Dad, I'm here."

"Hi, hon. I'm glad you made it," he said in a mere whisper.

Danielle asked if she could have a few minutes with him.

As soon as the family left, Danielle grabbed her father's hand and said, "Dad, do you know that I love you?"

"Yes, hon. We're good," he said.

"No, Dad. I love you. I want you to know that I forgive you for everything and I love you as you are. I want you to know that, Dad. I forgive you, and I know you did the best you could."

"We did all right, I guess," he said softly.

"No, you did more than all right. Look, I turned out great. Although we didn't always agree, you taught me to work hard and you made me tough."

"You are tough," he said with a grin.

"Yes I am, Dad. And, I want you to know..." tears were flowing too heavily and she had to stop so she could catch her breath. "Dad, I want you to know that I completely forgive you. For anything and everything. I don't want you to leave this world without knowing that I have forgiven you. I don't expect to have a conversation about our past, but I want you to know that I am your daughter and all I ever wanted was for you to love me. Before you head off to heaven's pearly gates, I want you to know in no uncertain terms that I hold only love for you in my heart, Dad."

Danielle could barely breathe. She let the words leave her mouth as a gift-wrapped package filled with love.

"I love you too, hon," her dad said smiling. Danielle sensed it was difficult for him to accept the gift she freely gave.

"So, we're good, Pops. We're good." Then Danielle kissed him on the forehead and sent as much love as she could through to him. Soon his breathing grew shallow, so for the next hour or so she sat there holding his hand. After a while, the hospice nurse came in and checked his vitals and looked at his feet.

"There's some mottling on his legs and his respiratory rate has fallen. It won't be long now. Can I bring your mom and brothers back in?"

"Of course," Danielle said.

The rest of the family came in and stood around his bed, saying sweet words, telling a few jokes and holding his hands and feet. About an hour later, he took his last breath and it was over.

CHAPTER
14

A year later, Danielle was given the biggest shock of her life. She walked out of the CEO's office, stunned. She'd been fired. A "corporate restructuring" he'd called it, but she knew what it was. "I've never been fired," she whispered as she got into her car and drove away bewildered.

Her ego was bruised. As the consummate overachiever, she was driven by success, always achieving, always striving for more. "Now what?" she wondered.

It took several weeks to recover. Her employees as well as peers contacted her, asking if she was "OK." Danielle responded to each inquiry with the same message, "This is happening for a reason, and I trust that amazing things will come from it."

Danielle believed it – sort of. Yet, her heart ached. She was convinced this job had been part of her destiny: the significance for which she'd been searching.

After selling her business, she chose this company because

of her belief in its products. And although she didn't enjoy working for someone else, Danielle was passionate about the work, loved the people she worked with, and felt like she was making a difference.

She picked up one of her favorite books by Iyanla Vanzant and opened the page to a sentence that almost knocked the wind out of her lungs, "Rejection is God's protection," it said. "When God closes a door it means it's time to move in a new direction."

"OK, now what? If that wasn't the reason I am here, what is?" Danielle mused restlessly.

Weeks later, there was still no answer.

Danielle secretly believed she needed to start her own business, but didn't want the stress she had experienced with her consulting company. She wanted to own a business not because of the control it offered, but the freedom it carried: to make decisions that were in the best interest of customers and employees, and not shareholders or board members. She had forgotten what a luxury it was to be free to think outside the box, without having to make futile attempts to impart ideas to those unable to see beyond the box. That kind of creative thinking was the most exciting form of freedom she craved.

Danielle knew one thing: she wanted to focus on helping other people and not build a business for the sake of making money. Suddenly, she remembered something her grandfather said when she was a kid, "God will show you the way, but you have to make the way."

"OK God, show me the way," she prayed. "What is the way, God?"

She remembered a scene from her childhood, something tucked away that she'd never told anyone, partly because she wasn't sure if it really happened, and partly because she was fearful it might be true.

She closed her eyes. Danielle remembered that an angel had

visited her one lonely night in her dad's van when her brothers were sleeping. The angel told her she was here for a reason. She had always cherished that dream, sensing that she was on this Earth for a specific reason. It seemed like everything she had tried, from mentoring others to starting her own business, had certainly helped people, but it never felt like she was making the kind of difference her soul ached for.

The next morning, Danielle awoke with the memory of the personal mission statement she'd written many years ago as part of a workshop. She jumped up and hurriedly dug through the drawer, looking for the crumpled index card. Finally she found it and read the words out loud:

"My purpose is to inspire people to achieve their potential."

Danielle wasn't sure how to realize that calling, but had a nagging sense that this phrase held the key to her destiny. Hopeful, she looked up her old mentor, David, and asked him playfully if he was still available to give sage advice.

"Ha! For you? Anything, my dear!" David exclaimed. "And what have you been up to? The last time we talked, you had a training company called 'Succeed on Purpose' if I recall. Great name, by the way."

Danielle explained how Succeed on Purpose had morphed into a 40-person marketing consulting company, and that she hated the work, so she sold the company prior to the recent recession. Then she took a chief marketing officer position and although she really enjoyed the company, it didn't work out either. She shared with him the personal mission statement she'd recently found in her drawer and finished with, "And now, I don't know what to do."

"Wait a minute," David said. First, you turned your training company into a marketing consulting firm, Danielle?"

"Uh, yes..." Danielle said as she stammered around trying to explain about profits and growth, but her words were hollow.

"And your mission statement, or better yet, your purpose statement, is to inspire people to achieve their potential?"

"Yeeesss...," Danielle answered uneasily.

"I thought Succeed on Purpose meant you succeed while working on and in your purpose. Your life purpose. Danielle, your purpose is to inspire people to achieve their potential. That's where success lies," David said emphatically.

There was silence on the other end of the phone.

Danielle thought to herself, "How could I have been this stupid to..." and caught herself. "No, I am not stupid," she said to herself. "I missed an important point, that's all."

"Danielle, are you there?" David asked, interrupting the conversation she was having with herself in her head.

"Yes, I am. David, as crazy as it sounds, I missed that point. I thought Succeed on Purpose meant to do it deliberately. All of our training programs were about strategy and process. It didn't occur to me it was about my purpose," Danielle said flatly.

David spoke intently: "Success is not the same as purpose. Success isn't about planning to be successful, but being truly purposeful about it. True fulfillment comes when you know your purpose in life and align everything to build a life on that purpose."

"I see," Danielle said, still in shock. She'd always put success first, never thinking about purpose. To her, success meant things like winning, money, respect. But those things never fulfilled her in the way she ached for now.

"But, how can I build a business on that, David?" Danielle asked quizzically.

"I don't know, but if anyone can figure it out, you can," David added.

Danielle knew he was right. She would figure it out. For the next several weeks, she talked to friends as well as previous employees and customers, asking if they knew their purpose in life. They all responded, "No, but I wish I did."

Finally, her best friend Patricia asked, "Danielle, do you think you can show me how to find my purpose?"

Danielle said, "Sure. It's easy. All you do is..." and within three minutes she had helped Patricia find her purpose statement.

"Danielle, that's amazing!" Patricia exclaimed. "I know lots of people who would pay for that kind of clarity!"

"Really?" Danielle asked incredulously.

"Heck yeah! I've developed personal mission statements and personal brand statements, but it never felt right. What you did, well, it felt like a tuning fork for my soul," Patricia added.

Danielle was silent. The magnitude of Patricia's words washed over her. "A tuning fork for your soul...," Danielle mused.

Patricia added, "What if you could help people find their purpose in life first, and then help them build a business, career or life around that purpose?"

Danielle knew her purpose was to inspire others to reach their true potential, and that she had a gift for truly seeing others, not only as who they were today, but for the potential they had inside for success. She knew she could help show them that potential – hold it up to them like a mirror – and help them find their way.

"But how?" she wondered out loud to Patricia.

"I don't know, but if anyone can figure it out, you can," Patricia said encouragingly.

Danielle knelt down next to her bed and prayed for God to show her how to build a business around this purpose concept. After a few minutes, she heard softly, "You get what you focus on, Danielle."

"Gramps, is that you?" Danielle could feel his presence in the room. "I don't know what to do. I want to help people, but I don't know how."

The words came again, this time louder: "You get what you focus on."

Danielle knew the key to her grandfather's phrase was to focus on what she wanted -- her purpose. She picked up her pen and wrote:

> *Purpose answers the question, "Why am I here?" My purpose is to inspire people to achieve their potential.*
>
> *My business and life goals can be aligned with that purpose. Goals answer the question, "What can I do to fulfill my purpose?"*
>
> **My goals then are:**
>
> *1)   Teach people how to find their purpose.*
>
> *2)   Teach people how to overcome fear, build confidence and build a plan to LIVE that purpose, both personally and professionally.*

She could feel a sense of clarity wash over her, but it was soon replaced with doubt. "But how?" she wondered.

Right about that time, with doubt starting to fill every crevice in her mind, she remembered a sermon from her favorite pastor. He said God doesn't give us the "how" in the way we're accustomed to: in project plans, manuals or business plans.

Instead God gives us the "how" in little stepping stones, each step preparing us for the next, and leading us from where we are to where we're supposed to go. Her pastor said, "everything happens for a reason." She thought about how various events in her life had led her from one place to another and how true this statement was for her.

So, she drew a diagram of her life up until that point, calling it a "Life Board." She outlined all of the major things that had happened and what she had learned from each challenge. She was amazed. Her Life Board looked exactly like stepping stones!

She could see it all very clearly now. She probably wouldn't be alive today if Coach Dabney, her favorite guidance counselor, had not talked to her at practice. Had she not left home, she might not have made it to college. If she hadn't graduated college, she wouldn't have had professional success. If she hadn't abused her body through her excessive work habits, she wouldn't have discovered how her beliefs translated to actions. And, if she hadn't been fired, she would have continued to do what she was "good at," not what she was destined to do: "inspire people to achieve their potential." It felt good every time she said it out loud.

"Gramps, thank you for guiding me through those early years," she whispered. "You were always there for me. You were my guardian angel on earth. In fact, there were lots of angels. They always showed up exactly when I needed them."

"Stepping stones," she said. "That's how I'll figure it out: One step at a time."

The angel that sat next to her smiled and said, "Well done."

SECTION THREE

PEACE: Build a Life on Purpose

CHAPTER
15

BUILD A LIFE ON PURPOSE

Five Lessons of Peace

Before we begin the process of teaching you to find your purpose, I want to point out a few critical lessons you'll need for your purpose journey. I call them the "Five Lessons of Peace," because that's what they've given me – peace on my purpose journey.

The story you just read is my story. It's written in realistic fiction, because what happened, when it happened or how it happened isn't important. What matters is what we do with what happens. Everything else is just a perspective in time.

That's Lesson 1: What we do with what happens to us.

Whether your life has been as challenging as mine, or whether you had great parents who nurtured you isn't the issue. Everyone has wounds from childhood. The question is not what happened to us, but what we choose to do with what happened.

Who knows what I would have become had my birth family raised me. Although I believe that every woman has a right to choose when faced with the complicated decision of bringing a child into this world when she is only a child herself, there is no way to predict whether things would have been better or worse. I certainly fantasized about what it would have been like to have grown up with my birth family. So much so, that I spent 11 years looking for them, and at 29 years old was reunited with both birth parents.

It was a beautiful experience, but it didn't change who I was. All it did was help me to better understand myself and the people who gave me life. And, best of all, it gave everyone peace to know that I had turned out fine.

Although I am part of their family today, and they a part of me, I do not consider them my "parents." Why? Because despite all of their issues, the Freys parented me the best they could. No parent is perfect, and I believe that we can learn as much from ineffective parenting skills as we can from having loving parents. Either way, life is a process and we get to choose what we make of it. Most importantly, my life was indeed exactly as God had planned.

That's Lesson 2: Everything happens for a reason.

For the most part, I needed those difficult years to find the compassion that now is the foundation of my life. I needed the pain in order to learn to live a life of faith. I needed to learn how to survive in order to learn how to thrive. I needed agony to find peace, and I needed to have angels and guides in order to learn how to soar. And yes, I needed tragedy in order to find purpose.

Which brings me to Lesson 3: Everyone has a purpose.

I've learned that there are a lot of people hungry for purpose in their life. And like me, they know they are here for a reason, but are afraid to discover what it is. Most of us think that if we focus too much on God's purpose for our lives, He'll ask us to become a monk or join the Peace Corps. But that isn't how God works. God calls us to use our strengths and passions for His purpose. God knows that I don't like bugs so he's not going to ask me to travel to the Amazon or

Belize to work in the jungle. He wants for me what I want for me. And now that I have built a business on my purpose, work doesn't feel like work, and success is the cherry on the top, not the focus.

And, of course, Lesson 4: Success is not the same as purpose.

You should know by now that you get what you focus on. The question is, what are you focused on? Success or purpose? There is a difference, and when you are "on purpose" is when you will find true success.

And finally, Lesson 5: Angels and guides are everywhere.

Before we begin to uncover your purpose, believe that you have angels and guides too. They are everywhere if you take the time to look and listen. They are in books, movies, workshop leaders, preachers, neighbors, co-workers, friends and family members. They are people who showed up at the right time, with the right information or encouragement, to help you move to the next stepping stone.

Regardless of your journey to this point, your challenges were not there to punish you, but to prepare you to live your purpose. And, the time for your purpose has come.

Everyone has a purpose. Everyone. As I said when I started the book, my purpose is to help you find yours. And the final chapter is dedicated to doing that.

CHAPTER
16

FIND YOUR PURPOSE; CHANGE YOUR LIFE

Everyone has a purpose. Everyone. At Succeed on Purpose, Inc., our job is to help you find yours. Your job is to remain open.

You've probably known a friend or colleague who was living a life perfectly suited for that person. Maybe you've been envious or maybe you tried to model their life in some way. Regardless, if you've ever felt that you weren't where you were supposed to be, consider opening yourself to a new path.

Through our workshops and DVD series, we invite participants to journey forward using what we call the Purpose Flow Chart™. The Purpose Flow Chart is part map and part structural drawing. More importantly, it's completely inspired by a divine spiritual process that I've personally used to find success and significance.

The Purpose Flow Chart has three steps that must be discovered in a specific order: Purpose, Goals, and Mission. The process will bog down if you try to move ahead too quickly, so stay focused on each individual component and don't move ahead until you're ready. The Purpose Flow Chart maps out a path to help you understand why you're here, what you could be doing to live that purpose, and how to order your life so that your purpose becomes a reality.

Each step of the Purpose Flow Chart asks a fundamental question, and has an end result that will guide you through the next part of the Purpose Flow Chart.

THE 3-PART PURPOSE FLOW CHART™

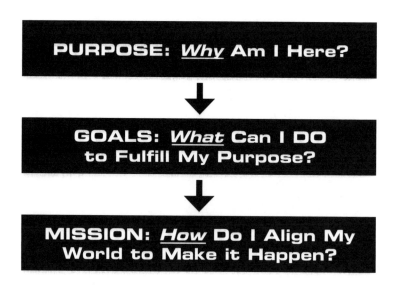

The first step of the Purpose Flow Chart is PURPOSE. Purpose answers the fundamental question, "Why am I here?" I sincerely believe that every person has a distinct purpose and their soul is on this Earth to accomplish something important in the overall scope of the human race.

Purpose can be considered your central "theme for life." When a soul is "on purpose," it will feel "in tune," which is why many of our workshop participants refer to the Purpose Exercise as a "tuning fork for the soul."

Purpose is made up of two things:

Strengths: Since God would never ask us to do something we aren't already good at, strengths play a major role in purpose definition. Strengths come from our brain, and should be considered those things that we, as well as those close to us, would say are unique talents.

Passions: Equally important, God would never ask us to do something that we aren't passionate about either. Passions come from our heart. We feel our passions, whereas we think about our strengths. If you have trouble getting in touch with emotions, finding passions might be difficult.

Instructions on finding your purpose:

1. Write down 10 strengths. What are you really good at? You may list personal or professional strengths.

2. Rank them (and re-rank), with No.1 being the best strength.

3. Second, write down 10 passions. What do you love doing so much that it seems effortless? You may list personal or professional passions.

4. Rank them (and re-rank), with No. 1 being the most passionate.

5. Circle words from both lists where you sense ENERGY. Energy can be felt, heard, sensed. Choose carefully.

6. Once you have the list, try to arrange the words into a purpose statement. You'll know when you've found it because it will feel like a tuning fork for your soul.

Here's an example from my own list of strengths and passions:

STRENGTHS:	PASSIONS:
1. Strategic	1. Inspiring People
2. Good Listener	2. Speaking/Training
3. Inspiring/Leading	3. Travel
4. Great Speaker	4. Writing
5. Marketing Expert	5. Meditation/Prayer
6. Passionate	6. Family
7. Training Others	7. Great Food/Wine
8. Make the Complex Simple	8. Music
9. Writing	9. Leading Others
10. Fitness/Exercise	10. Beach

To develop a Purpose Statement draft, find one action verb that has the most energy from the list. If you see the same word on both lists, that's usually a pretty good indicator. In my case, "inspiring" shows up on both lists, and has energy associated with it for me. So I would start my purpose statement with "To inspire…" The next step is to ask "what/whom?" So I would say "To inspire what or whom?" The answer for me was people. Here are some possible purpose statements from the list above:

1) To inspire people
2) To inspire leaders
3) To lead with inspiration

There really isn't a "right way" or "wrong way" to do this exercise. If at any time you get stuck, you can email us at ican@ succeedonpurpose.com and we'll give you some suggestions via email for free! You're also welcome to join one of our workshops occurring around the country by visiting the **Products** page of our website, **www.succeedonpurpose.com**. And, if you'd like to host a workshop in your town and can gather at least 25 friends who also want to take the workshop, you can contact us at **ican@succeedonpurpose.com** and we'll work with you to book a Purpose Workshop in your town.

A FEW INSIGHTS ON PURPOSE:

Through our work in helping thousands of people find their purpose, we've noticed a few trends that we have turned into insights. These are guidelines, and we hope they will stimulate thinking about your direction.

1. Look at the list of strengths and passions: If there are more than eight (out of 20) items that are personal (travel, family, etc.), it means either that:

    a. You are out of balance right now (working too much), or

    b. Whatever you do, "balance" is a key component and your soul desires a life on purpose that includes balance

2. Look specifically at your strengths and passions. How many "line up" with what you are doing today? If there are more than eight (out of 20) that are significantly different from what you're doing now, it probably means your purpose will take you another direction.

3. If you struggled with your list of "strengths," you're probably struggling with confidence. If you struggled with your list of "passions," you're probably denying yourself good.

Now that you've found your Purpose, you're ready to move to the next step. Remember to take *ONE STEP AT A TIME!* Don't worry about *what* you'll do to fulfill your purpose, until you've figured out *why* you're here. The same goes with the second step in the Purpose Flow Chart: don't worry about *how* you'll live your purpose, until you know *what* you can do to live it!

Once you know your purpose, the next step is to determine

Goals. Goals, in this case, are not specific or measureable, but rather are broad-purpose goals. The main question for this part of the Purpose Flow Chart is: What can I do to fulfill my purpose? Remember, stay with the "what" and ignore the "how" for now!

Another word of caution: fear will most likely block you during this step. We spend a lot of time in our workshops getting fear out of the way. For now, know that fear is the only thing keeping you from living a life of purpose. It's up to you to decide whether you will let fear control you, or if you will control your own life.

Whereas the goals are still somewhat broad, they are not a theme like purpose. Goals are closer to being more tangible. Goals answer the question: "What can I do to fulfill my purpose?" Because this can be the most difficult part of the Purpose Flow Chart, it's helpful to brainstorm with other people who know you, as well as those who don't.

Most people find during this exercise that they will lose focus on "what" and start saying things like: "Yeah, but how will I do that?" If that happens, suspend disbelief and keep the focus on "what."

I think of this exercise as "brainstorming with God" (or whoever your higher power may be). I like to make a list of all of the broad goals for what I could be doing to fulfill my purpose. I encourage you to think outside the box! Remember, you are suspending your disbelief and concerns for the time being! Create as many options as possible. You might also want to brainstorm with another person; our workshop participants find this extremely helpful.

WHAT (BROAD GOALS):

1. Help people find their purpose
2. Connect people to resources
3. Teach people about health
4. Travel abroad and _____
5. Author books (general)
6. Start a virtual assistant business

HOW (SPECIFIC ACTIONS):

1. Write a book about purpose (specific book)
2. Develop a workshop on health
3. Build a plan to...

Again, since God would never ask us to do something we don't want to do, trust what comes up during this exercice.

When creating options for Purpose Goals, remember that there are NO "how" limitations! During this exercise, you are Superman®/Wonder Woman® and can do anything! Everything is an option to consider at this point.

Once you've developed at least seven broad goal possibilities, rank them in terms of the goals that would be easiest to implement. Since most people can't make radical changes at once, we suggest you take steps toward your purpose by incorporating at least one of your goals every few months.

Once you've answered the "what" question, it's time to align your Mission: How will you align your world to live a life of purpose? This is Step 3 in the Purpose Flow Chart: Mission Alignment.

Before I talk about mission, it's important to note that the primary thing preventing any of us from living a life of purpose is fear -- specifically, fear of failure.

To get the energy and motivation to change course and align with your purpose, you must identify fears holding you back.

A few tips:

1. Failure is not about winning or losing. Failure is a perspective taken at a point in time. If you look up the definition of failure in Webster's Dictionary it defines failure as: "Failing to perform a duty or expected action." Notice it says nothing about outcome! The only thing you can control is your actions. You can't control the outcome. Therefore, you only fail when you don't do the work (the actions you commit to). The outcome is completely out of your control.

---

[1] Superman and Wonder Woman are registered trademarks of DC Comics.

2. Fear is perfectly normal. Success doesn't mean you won't feel fear. Success is feeling fear and choosing to move forward anyway.

3. The two best remedies for managing fear of failure: Have a purpose and a plan! When you're "on purpose," you will be more willing to take risks because you will know you're doing what you're supposed to be doing.

4. Don't be afraid of being wrong. "Wrong" is really a guidance system during the purpose journey. When you move towards something that isn't right, "wrong" will get you back on course!

5. Learn to recognize fears and to manage them (rather than fears managing you!).

One other piece of critical advice: "How" doesn't come in a business plan, project plan OR a manual. Instead, it comes in pieces, kind of like stepping stones. Each step in the plan prepares us for the next. I find this part of the Purpose Journey the most difficult. My personality is that of a planner. I excel at planning, plus I always prefer to know where I am going. Unfortunately, to live a life of purpose, I have to give up the need to know where I'm going!

The good news is that we have developed a fabulous technique in the Purpose Flow Chart that will fake your ego into thinking it knows where it's going. Consequently, this will make the stepping stones a much easier journey.

Mission Alignment has three parts:

1. Give the ego a clear picture of where it's going, and align the vision you have for how to get there with your goals and purpose.

2. Decide what actions to take each week/month to move forward to that vision.

3. Make adjustments to actions (what you can control) to more closely align with your vision of how you want your life to be one year from now.

To align with your mission requires aligning three parts of your ego: your physical world, your mental world, and your emotional world. This will create a roadmap that will keep the ego focused on where you're going, while your soul spends its time focusing on how to move forward in the next step.

Go back to your Purpose and Goals. Now, imagine what life will be like a year from now, when you're living on purpose. Be very specific as you write out the following:

- Physical Alignment: What will my life be physically like a year from now when I am "on purpose?"

- Mental Alignment: What will I be thinking a year from now when I am "on purpose?"

- Emotional Alignment: What will I be feeling a year from now when I am "on purpose?"

Now that you've aligned your physical, mental and emotional world to your purpose, and your ego has a clear picture of where it's going, it's time to build your action plan. That's part 2 of Mission Alignment.

I prefer to do this with God as my "CEO," but you can choose to do this with your spouse, a friend or a coach. Make sure to determine who your CEO will be, and to determine a planning increment: either weekly or monthly. I schedule a monthly planning session during which I review my physical, mental and emotional alignment and I list the actions I will take in the next month.

At the end of each month, I have another session to evaluate my progress made from the previous month, and then make a new action plan for the next month.

Repeat this process for 12 months consecutively or until your world aligns to what you described in Mission Alignment.

As I said earlier in this chapter, there really isn't a right or wrong way to do the Purpose Flow Chart. If at any time you get stuck, you can email us at ican@succeedonpurpose.com and we'll give you some suggestions via email for free. You're also welcome to join one of our workshops occurring around the country by visiting the Products page of our website, **www.succeedonpurpose.com**.

And, if you'd like to host a workshop and can gather at least 25 friends who also want to take it, you can contact us at **ican@succeedonpurpose.com** and we'll work with you to book a local Purpose Workshop.

It has been an honor to serve you on this journey! All of us at Succeed on Purpose hope that you decide to take a step toward a life on purpose. One step is all you need and the first step is to begin!

Blessings and peace,

Terri Maxwell, CEO
Succeed on Purpose, Inc.

---

[1] Superman and Wonder Woman are registered trademarks of DC Comics.

About the Author

Terri Maxwell has been a successful business owner and marketing executive for 25 years. Her company, Succeed on Purpose®, is a unique "purpose driven" business incubation firm. Succeed on Purpose teaches participants how to find their purpose. When that purpose involves a business, Succeed on Purpose will assist with launching the new business concept through a "Business in a Box" program or its Business Incubation Services.

Terri has personally launched over twenty successful businesses and has coached hundreds of entrepreneurs to a six-figure income in their own business. Succeed on Purpose has transformed thousands of lives around the country with its "Find Your Purpose – Change Your Life" workshops. These workshops are effective because they provide actionable strategies, as well as a powerful FREE 1-year support program for participants.

Prior to launching Succeed on Purpose, Terri led Prodigy Communication®'s Internet marketing subsidiary to record-setting growth in the 1990s. In 2002, she started her own 40-person marketing consulting firm – LATIMARK® – which serviced some of the largest brands in the world; companies such as Target, Nokia, Texas Instruments and 7 Eleven.

She also built three successful sales organizations, and was named one of the top female leaders in the direct selling industry. Terri is a well-known motivational speaker and a transformational specialist. She graduated with honors from University of Texas at Dallas' MBA program in 2004 and obtained her B.S. from Indiana University SE with honors in 1987.

She lives in Dallas, Texas with her dachshund, Max.